Lions & Tigers & Babies!

Oh My!

one mom's journey through
the first year of motherhood

AMANDA H. YOUNG

ISBN 978-0-9833390-0-7

To Grandpa's Laughter
Cousin Ted's Morals
My Better Half, Rick
& the Amazing Ada

What's Where?

Introduction & Disclaimer

This is the story of a new mom's journey through the first year of motherhood. It doesn't start until my daughter, Ada, is already three-months old since it took me that long to realize we were all going to be just fine and that writing about life as I now know it would be therapeutic. Sometimes it's funny. Sometimes it's me preaching my opinions on things. Sometimes it's observations I've made from my new perspective on life as a mother. My hope is that it brings a smile to your face and, occasionally, a good laugh to your belly.

The cast of characters is real. The names haven't been changed. And my grammar isn't always perfect. If you're willing to accept that, please read on.

These are my personal experiences, based on my research, professionals I've consulted, things that have worked for me, and advice from friends. Don't just take my word for it if you see something here that piques your interest. Look into it further to see if it might apply to you. And note that I am just a new mom like all of the other new moms in the world. My formal training is in marketing and business administration. I have an MBA but no credentials in anything mom-related other than instinct and common sense. So what the heck do I know?

Moral of the story: I'm not an expert. Take from this book what you will and leave the rest.
Enjoy.

Our Story

My husband Rick and I met back in high school and our parents still live in the same hometown. After being good friends for many years, we finally started dating in college. We did the long-distance thing for a year or two since I went to the University of Iowa and he stayed at home while attending Northern Illinois University. It didn't take long for us to realize we were meant to be together. We got married when we were twenty-two, about two years after graduation.

We lived in Milwaukee for a few years during graduate school, Rick for Architecture and me for Business Administration. Then we took a leap of faith and moved to Chicago without having jobs but with the generosity of relatives giving us a deal on rent. That is when I first learned that you sometimes just need to wing it and hope for the best. We ended up with "real jobs" six months later.

Having started our careers and feeling a bit more settled, we decided to buy a condo. That was something we wanted to check off the list before having kids. Fifteen months later we had our daughter Ada and officially started our family at age twenty-nine, once we finally felt "ready".

In our travels through life, I've always taken on a role of being the one my friends look to for advice. My mom has been telling me to write a book filled with my common sense "wisdom" for years. I'm not sure I have collected enough wisdom just yet so instead of doing that book, I started taking notes on life as a new mom. This is the so-called "wisdom" I've gathered so far with hopes that by sharing what I've learned I might save another new mom from a similar, often embarrassing, fate.

Read on and (hopefully) wisen.

March

Frozen Car

For the first time in motherhood, I actually thought to myself "Now I know why people move to the suburbs."

Why?

A simple errand to the Social Security office to get Ada's Social Security card and number was much more than "simple".

After feeding, changing, and dressing her, securing her into her car seat while she was screaming at me no less, I zipped up the Bundle Me to keep her warm, put a hat on her head, and proceeded to gather the paperwork I needed to take with me. All of which was relatively normal.

Then I got my hat, gloves, and coat on. I moved her out our front door and into the hallway. I realized I had my house sandals on and quickly changed into my shoes. She was not screaming at that point so life was alright. In lieu of the cumbersome stroller, I decided to just take the car seat and the

Baby Bjorn with a fat suit for the little munchkin to wear since I couldn't carry her very far in the car seat—my first mistake.

With the diaper bag over my shoulder, the Bjorn and fat suit in my left hand, the car seat with the baby inside in my right hand, I used my third imaginary hand to open the first vestibule door, then the second. We made it outside—big accomplishment.

Then we walked a block-and-a-half to the car since it was parked a bit far. I arrived at the car, arms throbbing from the pain of carrying a twelve-pound baby in a seven-pound car seat. I opened the back door of the snow-covered car (two inches with a layer of ice underneath), and snow fell into the car. I tossed the fat suit, Bjorn, and diaper bag into the car. Then I grabbed the car seat and baby, walked to the other side of the car, opened it, again had snow fall inside, and finagled the kid into the clicky thing. By this time she was screaming her little head off. I tried to calm her to no avail. Maybe she would shake it off...

I shut the back door, opened the front door, started the car, turned on the defrost, grabbed the brush and scraper and got started. I dusted off the car and scraped the ice, periodically checking to see if she was still screaming. She was. I took a break and tried to calm her. She sucked on my finger for a bit, then started screaming again. I thought I would try to get the car moving and maybe that would help. I finished cleaning off the front windshield and hopped into the front seat. She was still screaming.

I put the car in reverse and pushed the gas. Nothing. I put the car in drive and pushed the gas. Nothing. Reverse again. Still nothing.

It was three in the afternoon. I was twenty minutes from the Social Security office which closed at four. The car was frozen to its spot and needed to thaw or be dug out. The baby was screaming. I had the start of a scratchy throat and my water that I carried with me didn't taste very good.

That is when I gave up. I turned off the car, went to the back passenger side, got the diaper bag, the fat suit, the Bjorn, reached for the car seat and of course, the tube of breast milk from the diaper bag fell out and rolled into the gutter. I grabbed it, put it back in the diaper bag and reached for the car seat again. Then the tube of breast milk fell out, again. That time I grabbed it, forcefully shoved it and the other tube and the baby bottle down deep into the diaper bag, grabbed the car seat with the baby still screaming at me, set her down in the snow, shut the door, locked the car, and tried to ignore the people on the street staring at me with my screaming baby. Then I trekked all my crap back to the house, stopping once to catch my breath and shake out my throbbing arm muscles. I got to the front door, unlocked it, pushed it open with my head this time— somehow my magical third hand wasn't available anymore— and as I marched up the four stairs, the thought of a nice house in the suburbs with a driveway and only one front door came to me. I shook it off, unlocked the second vestibule door, maneuvered all of the stuff and the baby inside, opened the house door, shimmied through and of course... Ada was now fast asleep resembling the cutest little angel you had ever seen.

But that was not all. I retrieved the tubes of breast milk from the bottom of the diaper bag and noticed that, yes, of course, they leaked! That was when I pulled out every nasty word in my vocabulary and cursed the designers of the bottles at Medela who had the foresight to put "Breast Milk is Best" on the side of each little storage tube, but not enough sense to make sure that the bottle didn't leak the very breast milk that mothers treated like gold.

Moral of the story: Motherhood isn't easy, babies cry, design matters, and city living is hard—but worth it.

Social Security

In another attempt to acquire a Social Security number for Ada, I decided to venture to the Social Security office to re-submit the paperwork for overnight processing. After learning about a week ago that there was no record of the paperwork submitted from the hospital when Ada was born, and not being able to go to the Social Security office earlier due to the car being frozen to the street, this was the day we ventured out.

Strategically, I waited until Ada had her morning nap and was in a better mood for travel and adventure. She was fed, changed, and seemed pretty happy. As with every excursion, I

3

snuggled her into her car seat, packed the diaper bag, bundled up for the cold weather, and drug everything out to the car, through the front door, the inner vestibule door, down the four stairs, through the outer vestibule door, and out to the car which was conveniently located in front of our condo after having thawed the day before. This time, I got a little lazy and assembled the car seat and stroller in our condo first and then took it out to the car by myself. After almost spilling the baby, stroller, car seat, and diaper bag down the first four stairs, I realized this really was a two-person job and was happy to see two nice strangers exiting my building and willing to hold the outer door open for me as I struggled with all of my crap.

Okay. We got into the car. Not easy of course. First, I put the car seat in the back seat and locked it in place, then I stuck the diaper bag and the bag with all of the paperwork next to the car seat. Then I shut the door, collapsed the stroller and shoved it into the trunk, all while stabbing myself in the thigh with a random stroller wheel part which would form a nice bruise later.

I opened the driver's side door, and yep, she was screaming. But I thought if I got the car moving she would calm down. We were on the road and she was doing okay. We made it about half way to the Social Security office on the north side of the city and she got really upset. I could soldier on, or pull off to see what was going on. I pulled off and realized she was hungry. So what if I just fed her before we left. I squeezed into the back seat of my blue Honda Civic and pulled out the ever-so-handy boob. We sat for fifteen minutes as Ada enjoyed a mid-afternoon snack while people walking by wondered what I could possibly be doing sitting in the back seat of my car in front of Trader Joe's. After arousing a good deal of suspicion, it was time to continue toward our goal.

Back on the road, we were doing well. We got to the Social Security office and parked at a meter since the lot was full. I thought an hour would be enough. How long could this take, really? I opened the trunk, unfolded the stroller, got the car seat out, grabbed the diaper bag, struggled with my jacket since I wore too many layers and it was hotter than I expected, and dug deep to find quarters for the meter. It was one in the afternoon. I had the meter until two. Great.

We get into the Social Security office, took a number and started waiting. And waiting. We waited for an hour-and-fifteen minutes to be exact. Ada fussed a bit but overall was doing great. She slept while I held her and did some leisure reading. Final they called out A162. (The woman with A160 was complaining that they wouldn't call her number and once they finally did, she had fallen asleep in the front row of the waiting area and never woke up when they did call it, so she got skipped.)

Our number was up. I repacked Ada into her car seat in the stroller and approached the window with all of my paperwork completed and in order. I handed it to the woman behind the counter who took her time reviewing it. I explained that the information has already been submitted but that was mid-December and I still hadn't received my number even though they said I should have expected it in six-to-eight weeks. This was week eleven and my tax accountant said it was worth one-thousand dollars for me to get the number and file it with my taxes so I was a bit anxious to receive her number. The woman behind the counter smirked at me and said, "Her number was issued three days ago. Here it is. Her Social Security card should be in the mail and you should see it in about a week."

My jaw dropped. The steam whistled from my ears straight out of a cartoon. "Are you serious? I just sat here for an hour-and-fifteen minutes so you could tell me the number was already issued and I'm wasting my time?" I quickly gathered my things, took a deep cleansing breath, packed up the kid and headed for the door, all the while hoping that I didn't have a ticket on my car.

I got to the car, ticket-free, thank goodness. I repacked all my crap and the baby into the car and we were on our way to errand number two. We got about five blocks away and Ada started screaming. I pulled over, got into the back seat and realized this time she was dirty. So I changed her on my lap in the very cramped back seat of my blue Honda Civic. Mind you, the car seat was in the middle of the back seat so I was only working with a third of the seat and my feet were sharing space with the diaper bag. And as I was changing her, she peed. It happened every time. Once she was all cleaned up and re-diapered, I placed her back into the car seat and she started screaming again. I tried the boob. I fed her again as the sun beat down on us in the already hot car as sweat started collecting on the center of my back. After a fifteen-minute feeding session, we were on our way to errand number two, again.

Traffic on Lincoln Avenue was a nightmare. Stop and go, slow, slow, slow. I was cursing every driver in front of me since, even though I just changed and fed the baby, she was still not happy. Twenty minutes later, we were in front of Ada's new daycare ready to drop off her admission paperwork. There was no street parking so I double parked and threw on my hazards. I removed Ada from the car seat thinking it would be easier not to lug that thing around and half-heartedly wrapped her in my coat as I approached the daycare. Fortunately for the safety of the kids, the place was like Fort Knox. Unfortunately for me, I couldn't contact anyone inside or find anywhere to leave the paperwork where it would be secure. After three attempts at the buzzer and the back door, I gave up and we took a failing grade for errand number two.

Then we went back in the car for errand number three. We were heading to the doctor's office to drop off a form they needed to fill out for daycare regarding Ada's immunizations. Halfway to the doctor's office, Ada started hollering again. So I started hollering back and cursing more drivers to get out of my way and overall just started having my own personal little nervous breakdown. The phone rang. It was my husband. He made the mistake of asking me how I was doing. I explained that I was having a nervous breakdown, now wasn't a good time to talk and I would see him at home later. He wished me luck and I hung up. We arrived at the doctor's office. Again, I moved to the back seat of the blue Honda Civic to calm Ada. This time I tried to feed her. She had a cold that week and the boob seemed to be the best way to calm and comfort her. Poor little thing. After ten minutes, she was back to a more peaceful state. I re-latched the buckles of her car seat and drug her and the paperwork into the doctor's office. I dropped it off at the reception desk and headed back out to the car. We got settled in and set off for home. As we pulled out of the parking lot, Ada started in with the screaming again. I took a few more cleansing breaths and drove home as quickly as possible without doing anything too illegal. We finally got home, unloaded most of our crap as I decided to leave the stroller in the trunk for the night, dragged it all through the outer and inner vestibule doors and through the front door into the peaceful place we call home.

Moral of the story: Government systems are to be avoided at all costs, traffic in the city sucks, and trying to run errands with a small child recovering from a cold guarantees nothing but screaming.

Pharmacy Meltdown

It's a Monday, it is time to visit the doctor since Ada is still suffering from a cold and it's been over a week so the doctor wants to see her. Our appointment is at three, we have friends coming over at six fifteen, and we want to pick Daddy up from work after running errands at Target to get supplies for daycare. To the doctor's office we go, but not before prepping the diaper bag, packing the baby in the car seat, and dragging everything to the car via the front door, inner vestibule door, down four stairs, out the outer vestibule door and into the car. We skip the stroller this time knowing we will have the cart and won't be going far from the car.

Travel to the doctor's office is uneventful. Once we arrive, Ada is a bit fussy. She drinks from her bottle a bit as I struggle to show the receptionist my identification and insurance card which is the same as it was last week when I was here but they have to check every time "just to be sure." After waiting for ten minutes they finally call her name over her screams of discomfort. We're led back to the examination room and I'm asked to undress her. The nurse weighs her, says the doctor will be right in. We hang out and I feed her the rest of her bottle. She pees, I change her. The doctor comes in and examines her. That's a tough job when Ada screams while the doctor tries to listen to her chest. Finally the doctor decides to give her a prescription for Albuterol to help open her lungs a bit since she has some phlegm making it tough to breathe while she's eating. We're good to go.

Suddenly I remember the paperwork I dropped off on Friday and ask the doctor if it is completed and in her file or what the status is so I can submit it to her daycare.
"What form would that be?" asks the doctor.

"The one recording all of her immunizations that I dropped off on Friday and called you about."
"Oh, let me check," she replies.

Ten minutes later she returns to say they found it and she starts filling it out. She needs to get more information and says she'll be right back. Ada is doing well and we're playing. Ten minutes later the doctor returns and says she'll make a copy of the immunization information and we'll be ready to go. She'll be right back. Ten more minutes pass, Ada starts screaming because she's dirty, and I change her. Ten more minutes pass and finally a nurse comes in to say, "You're just waiting on this form right?"
"Yes."
"The copy machine back here isn't working for some reason so I'll take this up to the front desk to copy it and meet you there."
"Great."

The bundling begins. I settle Ada down, pack her into her car seat, repack the diaper bag, put on my coat, gather everything up and head to the cashier to pay my co-pay. The nurse meets me and hands me the paperwork that she finally photocopied as I glance at my phone. It is four thirty. Holy crap! I only have half-an-hour before I'm supposed to pick Rick up from work and we still have to go to Target and get Ada's prescription filled before company arrives at our house at six fifteen. I call Rick. He encourages me to head to Target and if he doesn't hear from me by five twenty-five he'll take the bus home and let our friends into our house.

Ada and I head to Target. And she cries most of the way there. I park and load her car seat into a nearby cart. With my list and coupons in hand, we hustle toward the pharmacy. We grab a few things on the way and Ada's level of fussiness starts to increase. As we reach the pharmacy counter, Ada enters into a full-blown meltdown. Nothing is working to calm her. She's screaming bloody murder as I'm trying to give the prescription to the pharmacist and explain that she has never had a prescription filled here before. The pharmacist fills out the necessary paperwork for me since my hands are full with a screaming child that is inconsolable at this point, and asks me to come back in twenty minutes. With Ada bouncing in my arms, I head for the Kleenex aisle and then to the elevator as we're off to the baby section. We grab a few things for daycare and are lucky to get the last box of Target brand un-scented bulk baby wipes. Back to the elevator, we return to the pharmacy. The meltdown returns. As I struggle to unload my cart with my free hand, the pharmacist is ringing up my purchases and trying to explain how I'm supposed to give Ada her new inhaler with the fancy contraption it attaches to as my phone is ringing.

I fumble for the phone as I dig out my coupons and pass the crumpled wad to the cashier while subsequently putting my credit card into the reader and trying to unsuccessfully wedge Ada back into her car seat. I ignore the call as it happens to be my friend, neighbor and regular pharmacist Kelly, who I'm sure knows that I am cheating on her with this Target pharmacist and will therefore think I'm a bad friend/neighbor/customer. Ada's meltdown continues as I am momentarily shocked by the $180 price tag of my quick target run, but I'm too busy to care as she is still screaming, the guilt for cheating on my pharmacist is mounting, and I'm trying to figure out if I'll make it home in time to greet our dinner guests. The wonderful pharmacist, her name was Beth, kindly steps around the counter to help load all of my purchases into my cart and send Ada and I on our way, or just get us out of her store.

We exit the Target and arrive at the car. I load everything into the back and Ada is still crying. It is five fifteen and I need to catch Rick before he gets on the bus so I can pick him up from work. As I start the car, I check my voicemail and learn that my friend/neighbor/pharmacist Kelly needs to borrow black pants for her trip to New York tomorrow. I try to return her call but get voicemail and leave a message saying she can have whatever she wants and can stop by anytime. I try to call Rick and get his voicemail. As I try again, he is calling me and I go to click Swap Call/Answer and hit Ignore instead and lose his call and my connection to his voicemail. At this point, Ada is screaming, I'm trying to drive in downtown Chicago, and I can't get Rick's stupid phone to connect. I'm screaming at Ada who's screaming at the world, when finally I connect with Rick and put him on speakerphone as I finish my tirade of insults I'm spewing at traffic at the light in front of me. Rick, unbeknownst to me, has been fighting a cold and has just ridden down the elevator from the thirty-fifth floor while his sinuses are draining to innocently answer the phone as I'm screaming into his ear that has yet to pop from the pressure in the elevator, resulting in a sharp pain that makes him wince. Poor guy. He quips back that I need to calm down and I explain that I'll meet him in five minutes at his building. Whew!

In route to Rick's office, Ada is screaming, I get stuck at every red light and behind every loading and unloading cab to be had, and the five minute drive seems like twenty-five minutes. I arrive and pull up to the curb for Rick to get into the backseat of our blue Honda Civic and what do I hear but... oh yes... silence. Daddy's here and all is well in the world as Ada passes out and doesn't utter a peep the rest of the way home.

Moral of the story: Pharmacists are some of the best people on Earth, patience is a virtue when visiting the doctor, and a partially sick child will make any errand nearly impossible.

ADA Compliance

With my mother in town for some quality time with her granddaughter, today is the day we venture to the Cheesecake Factory on Michigan Avenue via the good old CTA bus. We're scheduled to meet my brother and a friend at one thirty for lunch so we head out at one. Getting downtown is fairly easy.

The bus comes. I finagle the stroller halfway into the bus while my mom lifts the other end as we climb the stairs and get situated in the front area of the bus reserved for elderly, disabled, and parents traveling with small children. Somehow in the midst of getting onto the bus, I also manage to find my bus pass and swipe my card for two fares.

We arrive at our stop and have some difficulty getting the stroller off the bus as I catch a wheel on one of the railings on the stairs. Somehow we manage to get out without major incident and are on our way to lunch. After a nice leisurely stroll to Michigan Avenue, we arrive at the base of the Hancock building to meet my brother. It's one thirty-one and we're trying to figure out how to get the stroller into the Cheesecake Factory. I'm quickly scanning the scene for any sign of a handicap entrance or regular, i.e. non-revolving, door. My brother calls from the inside of the restaurant and asks where we are. "We're stuck outside. Can you ask someone how we get inside?"

For those of you who are unfamiliar with the Cheesecake Factory, it is located on the lower level of the Hancock building. There are two massive staircases leading down to the main entrance which is comprised of a few revolving doors and several regular doors, however the "regular" doors are all affixed with an emergency alarm system. There is also a small revolving door on the street level for their upper dining area. My brother meets us on the street level and we decide to collapse the stroller and shimmy in through the revolving door as one person takes the stroller and one takes the car seat. I am the smallest so I get the stroller. Thank goodness I'm tiny and I'm only a little claustrophobic because there would have been a major panic attack had I become stuck in this tiny door. After a brief moment of concern that I might not make it, the revolving door opens into the restaurant and I breathe a huge sigh of relief.

But not so fast. We aren't seated on the main floor. We're eating on the lower level since the main floor isn't open today. So I have to drag the stroller down a grand staircase with a seemingly endless number of steps. At the bottom, I'm ready to pass out since I've just lugged a twenty-two pound stroller all over the place and it's lunch time. Hello! I'm eating for two since I'm nursing and I'm starving! Finally we ditch the stroller at the hostess stand and are escorted to our booth for four. Seriously? You want four grown adults and a baby in a car seat to squeeze into a tiny booth when there is no room for a high chair in the aisle? Not going to happen. We request to be moved and are re-seated in what I call a "mobster" booth—the type the mob would sit in since it is huge and gives you a view of the whole restaurant. Once we're settled, things are going well.

We eat. We play pass the baby to stop her from fussing. I take her to the bathroom to change her. Thankfully this restroom does have the Koala Kare changing station on the wall of the handicap stall. However, the restroom isn't very clean, the music is really loud, and it's dark to set a romantic mood while you pee I guess. And while I'm ranting I'll point out that the lock for the handicap accessible bathroom is at my shoulder height. Now I ask you how someone in a wheelchair a) got into this damn building in the first place and b) can reach this deadbolt to lock the bathroom door. After changing Ada, I go to wash my hands and am surprised by the water temperature. It isn't just hot. It's scalding. There is steam rising from the basin of the sink. Talk about a lawsuit just waiting to happen. Uninjured, we make our way back to the table to finish my now cool lunch.

After dessert, this is the Cheesecake Factory after all, we ask how to get out of the building and the hostess tells us we can go into the observatory entry to get out. I don't think she ever really understood that we are trying to get out with the stroller in some kind of elevator. So again, we squeeze into the revolving door. At least this one is a bit larger, for which I am very thankful. Then we climb the grand staircase outside the Hancock building and say our goodbyes as my mom and I venture home.

I decide we should again ride the bus home because I don't really know how to take a baby in a cab. We'd have to strap down her car seat and load the stroller in the trunk and I think that would be a pain not to mention that I'm nervous about installing the car seat correctly as that is one of the main things they drill into your head in all of the baby classes and the media. In some delusion I have, I just assume the bus will be easier and cheaper ($4 versus $15 for a cab).

We get to the bus stop and wait. And wait. About ten minutes pass as my mom takes note of every available cab that passes us and finally the bus arrives. It is three thirty-ish. We're well before rush hour so this shouldn't be bad. But oh how very bad it is. I've got the stroller. My mom has Ada in the car seat. We climb onto the bus and I swipe my card for two fares again. Then I look up to see that all of the seats in the front of the bus are taken, by young, able-bodied persons no less, and NO ONE IS GETTING UP FOR US. Hello! Seriously? Discouraged with the human race occupying the front of this bus, I suck up my hurt feelings and raise the stroller above my head and squeeze through the crowd to the back of the bus. The VERY back of the bus. This means we have to go past the back door, up two steps, and find our seats. My mom follows with little Ada who's semi-asleep. As we are arriving at a set of available seats at the VERY back of the bus, the bus starts moving. Minor panic ensues. Since we haven't sat down yet, we all jolt forward, nearly falling over had it not been for a very strong and courteous angel on the back seat. This man quickly grabs my wrist and braces me as I start falling forward over the stroller. Doing so allows me to prevent my mom from falling as she leans into me with the car seat instead of completely face planting. I thank him profusely as does my mother while we try to get "settled" into our seats. Too bad you can't really "settle" into the seats at the back of the bus because they are arranged in a U shape where all of the seats back up to the walls so everyone's legs are in the middle. Unfortunately, that's where I've attempted to store the stroller. And I have the car seat on my lap, squishing my thighs quite uncomfortably I might add, while the stroller is digging into my leg every time we hit a bump or stop abruptly.

After about fifteen minutes on the bus, we arrive at our stop. Thankfully, the people that ride on the back of the bus are much more courteous than those that ride on the front (at least on this bus that is the case). I pull the cord to request the next stop and at least three of my fellow riders realize what's about to happen. During the fifteen minutes we've been on the bus, it has filled up nicely. There are riders packed body to body in the aisle and in the space in front of the back door. Just before we reach our stop I say, "This is us". As I speak up, my three fellow passengers also speak up to say "Mother and child coming out with a stroller. Make way." It doesn't make much of a difference right away but people eventually start to make room for us. My mom goes first to clear the way. I follow her and proceed to get something caught on one of the chairs and have the people behind me telling me I've dropped a baby bottle. Thankfully the gentleman we have just struck up a conversation with about how hard it is to live in the city with a baby, grabs the bottle, sticks it into the side pocket of my diaper bag and wishes me luck. After much effort, I make it to the doors to find two more gentlemen holding them open for me. My mom is on the sidewalk walking toward the front of the bus to thank the bus driver, since that's what nice people from small towns do, as I'm telling her she's going the wrong way to get to my house.

Finally we make it to my front door and what could be there waiting for us? None other than the outer and inner vestibule doors.

Moral of the story: When traveling with small children, always stand up for yourself even if it means potentially offending someone. When going about your daily business, be even more considerate of the elderly, disabled, and parents with small children as life makes everything a million times harder for them. And most importantly, teach you children to give up their seat on the bus or the El for Pete's sake!

Stupid Keys

I have previously made mention of the inner and outer vestibule doors in my building that are a giant pain in my backside since they make getting in and out of my building extremely difficult with a child. That was definitely the case this time.

The day started out well. Ada had her first transition day at daycare. She was there until two and decided she wasn't interested in having an afternoon nap. Once we arrived home, she was still fighting the idea of a nap so I fed her a bit. Normally that would be a simple task but I was pumping and feeding her a bottle at the same time since she wasn't hungry when I started—crazy I know.

So, there I was sitting at my computer desk, Ada in the bouncy seat next to me. The pump was at my feet. I had a tube top on that made the pump hands-free. I was pumping and had prepared a bottle for Ada in case she decided she was hungry mid-pumping. As she bounced away, the hunger cry began. I grabbed the bottle and fed her. I made the mistake of picking a burp cloth up off the floor to catch her dribbles and to my surprise, both pump containers leaked all over the floor. I lost about an ounce of milk because these stupid pump containers were not designed to resist gravitational forces when I leaned over. An ounce was a BIG deal in the world of breastfeeding. This stuff was gold remember. Oh, and since I liked to multitask, I was also on the phone with my husband saying, "Shit, Shit, Shit, I'll call you back. I'm spilling milk all over." Click.

We survived the milk episode but I was a bit spacey. "Pregnancy Brain" (overall forgetfulness and an inability to complete a thought while pregnant) didn't disappear with the birth of a baby. It just morphed into "Mommy Brain" and became a constant state of distraction. Ada was still not interested in taking a nap so I decided we'd venture out to run errands. We were expecting a hefty snow storm the next day so it seemed like a good time to seize the day and shop. Before motherhood, shopping was enjoyable. With child... not so much.

Fact of life: If you want to go shopping, you need to take a stroller.

As per usual, I bundled baby Ada into her car seat and took her out my front door and into the hallway. She started crying. I went back inside for the stroller thinking I would do this in phases. The shopping list, my coat and the diaper bag were next. Once in the hallway, I had this great idea to take the stroller to stage two, which was between the vestibule doors, and come back for the rest of the stuff. I opened the inner vestibule door and finagled the stroller through. As the stroller cleared the doorway, it started rolling down the stairs and I quickly grabbed it and placed it at the bottom of the stair clear of the outer vestibule door in case my neighbors needed to get in while I proceeded to phases three, four, five and six.

Then it hit me.

I had just locked my baby in the hallway of my building, while she was crying, and I didn't have keys to the vestibule door. I resisted the urge to panic and instead propped open the outer vestibule door and pushed every buzzer in the building as I prayed one of my neighbors was home. My chances were limited as I knew I was not going to buzz myself in and I was fish sitting for one of my neighbors who was in San Francisco so that left four options and it was three thirty in the afternoon. I buzzed. No one answered. "Shit, Shit, Shit." I buzzed again. Nothing. I took a deep breath, stepped outside (thank goodness it was the first day of spring and forty-five degrees out since I wasn't wearing my coat) and flagged down the first person to walk by my building.

"Hi. Can I borrow your cell phone? I just locked my child in my building and I don't have my keys."

"Sure," he said as I quickly called my husband and explained the situation.

"How can I get into our house?" I asked.

"Ummmm..." He replied.

Well, if I weren't so anal about locking all of the windows, I could have maybe pushed one open but I was on an elevated first floor so I'd have needed this random guy to help me out. Not gonna happen. Back door? Nope, it was locked too, and I didn't have a key to get into the fenced in area behind the house anyway. The Security Shop around the block had a copy of the key to the doors, but I couldn't leave the baby, and they surely wouldn't give it to this random guy who had helped me out. Not to mention it would have cost me $100 just for them to walk around the block and open the door. Instead, my husband said he'd grab a cab and be home in fifteen minutes. Okay. That would work. I was saying thanks and goodbye to my random stranger/hero when one of my neighbors miraculously appeared. And she had keys! Thank you God! I thanked her profusely for her well timed arrival and went inside to find that Ada was no longer crying after her two minute adventure alone in the hallway and was calmly looking around for Mommy. Of course when I went to see if she was okay, she started crying. Go figure.

Moral of the story: Babies need their naps, don't try to accomplish anything while a baby is crying, and (obviously) never walk out your front door without keys to get back inside.

Easter Travels

Talk about exhausting. I thought traveling from my hometown of Sycamore to Macomb each holiday was tough, and I typically wasn't driving. But doing it with a three-month old was excruciating. What is normally a three-and-a-half to four-hour drive turned into five hours of:
"Take the next exit."
"Wahhhhhh!"
"No, don't take the exit. She's sleeping."
"Damn. Take the next exit. She must be wet."
"What? Now we need gas? Seriously? But she's asleep. Can't we just coast on fumes for awhile and wave our arms out the windows like propellers?"

Our trusty blue Honda Civic did a beautiful job of transporting my family to see my Mom's side of the family for Easter. It was baby Ada's debut to the relatives on that side and boy were they ready to meet her. After five grueling hours in the car, for which we had to stop numerous times to change her in the front seat, fill up the gas tank, nurse her so I didn't explode, take food and bathroom breaks, and just plain stretch, we finally arrived at my aunt's house. She was waiting patiently on the porch in the cold to get a glimpse of the baby.

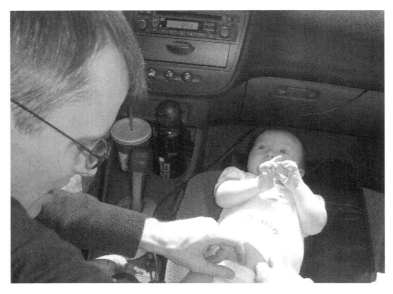

It was a calm but eager excitement. I unpacked Ada from the car seat and passed her off for the oohs and ahhs. Then came the necessities—we changed her diaper, fed her, and put on her Easter dress. We went with disposable diapers for this trip since we had a bag of size ones to use up before she outgrew them. But I'm a firm believer in the cloth diaper. (More on that later.) So we changed her, and changed her again.

Finally we headed over to my other uncle and aunt's house for Easter spaghetti dinner prepared by my grandfather. Again, oohs and ahhs and ogling. She was great and dinner went well. She posed for the paparazzi that is my family and my aunts took turns holding her during dinner. What a nice relief to be able to eat dinner at the same time as my husband while the food was still hot. Overall, the evening was pretty uneventful.

We stayed at my cousin's house. Ada started out in her Pack 'n Play but magically spent most of the night in our bed since she was gassy from what I could only guess was the mushrooms, garlic or tomatoes. I could never tell what foods I ate would make her unhappy later but my grandfather's spaghetti was definitely up there at the top of the list. But it was soooo good. Probably not worth losing that much sleep for, but oh well. I would know better next time.

Morning rolled around and it tried to snow. Some silly family member thought nine o'clock was an appropriate time for Easter brunch. We arrived fashionably late at nine thirty after my cousin loaded all of our stuff in the car, brushed off the snow and gave Ada her bottle while we frantically got ready. He's such a great guy.

At brunch we ordered and things were going well until Ada got fussy and had to be changed. My husband took the first shift. He returned and said, "At least the bathrooms are big so I had enough space to change her on the floor." Great. One of those. For those of us who have ever had to change a baby on the bathroom floor of a restaurant, we know it was never good. You never knew what was on the floor. You tried not to let the baby touch the floor at all but the changing pads that came in diaper bags were not very big and with the way babies squirmed it was difficult to avoid. Overall, it was a nasty experience and one that should be avoided. Just trust me on this one.

After five hours on the car ride home with more of the same wet, hungry, uncomfortable, sleepy, cranky baby, we made it back to the city just in time to park the car, unload all of our stuff, and pick up the house before heading to bed.

It's unfortunate that my mom's family is so far away. I'm thankful we get to see them a few times a year and even more thankful we don't have to do the drive very often.

Moral of the story: Avoid traveling with small children, avoid changing babies on the floor of public restrooms, and avoid marrying someone with a big family that is spread out all over the world if you plan to procreate.

Cloth Diapers—Beyond the Baloney

Parents magazine recently had some guy write an article about cloth diapers and boy did he ever bomb. His "source" was some clerk at a baby store that didn't help him much, and his research left much to be explained. So here's what I think you need to know in one quick read.

If you are like me – i.e. you want to keep it simple, are willing to invest a couple hundred dollars to get the right stuff and not have to mess with it all, don't want to break the bank, plan on having more than one child, and will be okay doing laundry every two or three days – then this is how you do it. If you aren't like me, this will probably be helpful anyway as you educate yourself about cloth diapers. And if you really don't want to become an expert in cloth diapers, consider this the cliff notes.

Let's begin.

There are all different types of cloth diapers and a whole new vocabulary to go with them. Here is what I feel you need to know.

Cloth diapers have two layers (for our purposes), an absorbent layer and a waterproof layer. One soaks up the pee and poo, the other keeps it in the diaper, hopefully. The absorbent layer (diaper) needs to be changed every time whereas the waterproof layer (cover) can be rinsed or just reused depending on its state post pee or poo. For overnight or long car trips, a "doubler" can be added to double the absorbency. A "doubler" is just an additional liner you put between baby and the diaper so they can wear it longer.

There are other options out there called All-in-ones (AIOs). They are a bit more expensive, used once before being washed so you need more of them, and they have an absorbent insert you put into a pocket. Some of them have fancy snap systems that grow with your baby so you only need to buy one size. Then tend to fit more snugly than the cloth diapers and covers that I use, thereby reducing saggy baby butt and the chance that the cloth diaper shifts in the cover potentially reducing leaks. It might be worth trying one or two to see if you like them before investing in a bunch. The increased cost was a deterrent for me.

There are also diaper services in which case you just pay them and tell them how much your baby weighs and how old they are so the service knows the diaper size and quantity to send to your home. They wash, dry, pick-up, and deliver the diapers. Again, this can be expensive.

I am a fan of pre-fold cloth diapers, sometimes called Indian/Chinese or Diaper Service Quality (DSQ) diapers. Who cares? Just go for the ones that are unbleached (Indian/more of a brown color instead of white) if you are given the option because they are softer and seem to be more absorbent. The difference between them is so minimal you should not stress over it. Supposedly the bleached ones last longer. Flip a coin or get some of each. Oh, and the reason they are called pre-folds is because they have more layers in the middle for absorption. You'll see them labeled as 4-6-4 meaning four layers on the sides, six in the middle. I think more layers would be more absorbent so look for 4-6-4 or 4-8-4.

For the covers, there are a ton of styles and even more fabric/color/pattern options. I recommend the Thirsties PUL covers (stands for polyurethane laminate if you must know). I've also tried Bummis Super Whisper Wrap and they don't have the inner leg gusset that prevents leaks except on the smallest sizes-- but they do have cute patterns. Their Super-Brite is better since it has the leg gussets.

My recommendation is that you get at least twenty-four pre-fold cloth diapers and six diaper covers that will fit your baby for each weight phase they enter. Since I'm trying to make this as simple as possible, here is one option (Note: I'm not being paid by anyone to say any of this stuff but if someone would like to pay me, I'd happily accept.)

Buy the following:

Diapers and Covers
For a newborn 6-12 lbs:
Six X-Small Thirsties Brand diaper covers
Twenty-four Small Chinese Pre-fold Cloth Diapers
Get the "natural" color cotton ones if possible as they are more absorbent and softer. I like the Indian pre-folds personally.

Note: If you are going to do a mixture of cloth and disposables, or only have one child, you might skip the X-Small covers and use disposables for the first six weeks since your baby could grow out of them that fast. They are also a lot more work and you might not want to deal with the extra laundry during your initiation as a new mom.

For a baby 12-20 lbs
Six Small Thirsties Brand diaper covers
Twenty-four Small Pre-fold Cloth Diapers—if you bought these for your newborn, you're all set.

For a baby 18-27 lbs
Six Medium Thirsties Brand diaper covers
Twenty-four Large Pre-fold Cloth Diapers

For a baby 25-40 lbs
Six Large Thirsties Brand diaper covers
Twenty-four Large Pre-fold Cloth Diapers—if you bought these already, they'll still work until you are ready to potty train.

Wet Bags
Two Small Wet Bags: A small wet bag for the diaper bag and a backup in case the one you need is in the laundry. (Ziplock gallon bags work too but we're trying to save the environment here so at least label and reuse them several times if you do decide to go that route.) I like the Bummis Wet Bags way better than the Mommy's Touch but I'm sure there are better bags out

there. Bummis have a drawstring closure whereas I'd recommend a waterproof closure but the Mommy's Touch fabric feels slimy and wet to the touch. I don't think either of them are all that "waterproof" for long periods of time but they both wash up nicely and really, they don't have to be perfect. They are just keeping the poo enclosed until you get home. And you can consider using them to transport wet swimsuits home from the pool once your kids are out of diapers.

Six Diaper Doublers
For overnight to prevent leaks, add a diaper doubler to baby's diaper for extra absorbency. You can do the same with AIOs. I found some at a local store on clearance. If you need a specific recommendation because you really want me to do all of the work for you, Kissaluvs Diaper Doublers are what I have and they work fine. I have four of them but would prefer to have six or eight since you never know when the last change is before the baby goes to bed and it is good to have a few backups in case you guess wrong.

Why these items you ask?
1) Because I said so.
2) To make little girls/boys like you ask questions (My father's answer to everything.)
3) If you must know, these covers are the best in my opinion because they are high quality, have the Velcro closures(no pins, no Snappis fasteners, no pulling the darn things up/down when they are covered in poo), have a fold-over laundry tab to latch the Velcro when you wash the covers so the Velcro lasts longer and doesn't get stuck on other laundry, and if you look at the leg holes, they have an inner elastic that holds snug to your baby's legs to prevent leaks, unlike other covers.
4) Because I married an architect and DESIGN MATTERS, DARN IT. Pay the extra couple of bucks to get something that doesn't suck. And just think about the money you're saving by not running to the store every other day for a pack of disposables.

Why six of each diaper cover?
It turns out that's how many I've needed or wanted to have. More would be great and I've tried to get by with less but when baby has a poop-filled day with five blowouts that slime each cover, you'll be glad you have six covers. And only six covers should do as long as you are lucky enough that your baby

doesn't have a lot of blow outs and you can reuse them. I tend to alternate them so that if she is wet, I switch to a different cover when I change her so I can let the wet one air dry and use it again next time. If you aren't cool with that, buy more covers, do laundry more often, put the baby in the next size up while you wash and dry one, or go rinse and dry them out between uses.

How do I wash them?
I recommend Charlie's Soap. You'll read once you get cloth diapers that you shouldn't use Dreft or other detergents as they will build up on the diapers. You can use Oxiclean once a week to strip them of any build up but don't use it more than that as it is said to strip the fibers. They also recommend Bio-Kleen, Seventh Generation or Ecover which can be found in grocery stores like Whole Foods. Don't bleach them as that will weaken the fibers and shorten their life span.

Why *Kellyscloset.com* or *cottonbabies.com*?
They have been good to me. My orders have been correct, timely, and they called to confirm something that was confusing on my order. The website is pretty good for a diaper website, and they have reasonable pricing, free shipping on qualifying orders and quantity discounts. I don't know Kelly, I don't have any affiliation with her. I found her site in the "Baby Bargains" book and liked it. Same with *Cottonbabies.com*. Feel free to shop around of course.

If your sole motivation for using cloth diapers is to save money, please account for the fact that daycares, preschools, and babysitters will likely use disposable diapers. Depending on how dedicated you are to using cloth, you might decide to use them while at home but use disposables when you go out. Just keep that in mind when calculating your savings. In reality, we tend to still use disposable diapers about 30% of the time for convenience, while the cloth diapers are being washed, when we have others take care of Ada, when she is sick or we are sleep deprived, and when we visit family or are away from the house overnight.

When you are done having kids, consider selling your diapers and covers or passing them on to a friend or someone in need. That's the true spirit of reduce, reuse, recycle.

Moral of the story: Cloth diapers take some getting used to, you need to educate yourself about them a bit, and the investment is upfront, but they make you feel good for keeping the disposables out of the landfill and that makes it all worth it. And they are really cute on baby's bottom.

April

Renovation

It is widely known that renovation is rarely easy. So why my husband and I thought it would be a quick and easy project to install a washer/dryer combo unit in our bedroom closet is beyond me. Way beyond me.

This all started when we had Ada and realized, (insert light bulb here), she soiled everything she touched and thereby increased our amount of laundry dramatically. And to compound the issue, we were trying to save money and the environment by using cloth diapers. Having one baby equaled three or four additional loads of laundry each week for us. My whole reason for even putting a washer dryer in our condo unit was that it would be better for resale, we would get the investment back when we sold our place, and it would be more convenient not to have to walk out the back door, climb down a flight of stairs, unlock the basement door and lug the laundry to the coin machines. My real breaking point was when one washer and one dryer out of the four machines downstairs decided to not work properly but continued to eat my hard-earned quarters. Five quarters per wash load to be exact. Then five more for the dryer.

I didn't last long without a washer/dryer in our unit. Ada was born mid-December and I made it to Valentine's Day—almost two whole months mind you. I researched different machines online and went with an LG WM3431HW that we purchased from Compact Appliance. It was an expensive piece of equipment, $1,300 after free shipping and the "romantic" holiday sale. It arrived just three days later, and became a conversation piece in our living room and then a night stand draped in plastic in our bedroom until it was installed.

Our first mistake was to assume we could install hookups in our closet by sprinkling fairy dust in our bedroom. It turns out that in reality it took our friend Martin and my husband a day to bump out the closet wall six inches, several nights of re-mudding the drywall, half a day for the electrician and a day-and-a-half for the plumber, and time for my wonderful husband to re-drywall, mud, sand, paint and re-install the closet organization system.

An inch of drywall dust later, (unfortunately they were out of fairy dust), we might have a running washer/dryer Tuesday evening, April eighth. Yes, that is just shy of two months later. Why? Because we thought our friend could do the plumbing, but it turned out to be way too complicated with a cast iron stack in the basement and no access to a vent pipe. Then we made the mistake of believing our plumber when he said he'd get us a quote. After three weeks of nagging him, the quote was $2,500! Ticked off from all that drama we called plumber #2 and he stopped by that day, quoted it on the spot, and started one week later for $700 less. Still way more than we expected but what could we do?

That is the background to the story. Let's zoom in on the day Plumber #2 came to visit.

April Fool's Day started out well. Rick called to say that the plumber would be calling sometime and may be stopping by to give us a quote. Awesome! Finally a responsive plumber. I was still in my pajamas feeding Ada when the plumber, Chuck, called. Mind you this was already my second pair of pajamas since Ada woke up that morning and threw up on me, down my cleavage and all over my pants at her first feeding.

Chuck said he'd come over at eleven to take a look. Fabulous! It was ten and Ada was a bit fussy. I got the wise idea of taking a quick shower before Chuck arrived so I would feel human and wouldn't smell like barf. I put Ada in her bouncy seat—which had no bounce as the batteries had died and Rick didn't have a chance to change them and I didn't have four hands or a clone to have done it either. I sat it in front of the bathroom door as I gathered clothes to wear and undressed for my shower. She started screaming the instant I was naked. Thank goodness the blinds were closed throughout the house as I picked her up, walked to her room and nursed her while naked. A few minutes later we tried again. She was still fussing in her bouncy seat when I jumped into the shower. I had fifteen minutes until he got here and could get ready in three so things were good.

I was showering when, of course, the phone rang. I quickly shut off the water, grabbed my towel, ran on tip toes past the screaming baby to the kitchen to get the phone, but it was in the living room. In one thousand square feet of condo, we had two cordless phones and a wall phone all in the living room. What were the chances of that? So I ran on tip toes to the living room, and soaked the floor along the way.
"Amanda, it's Chuck. I'll be there in ten minutes."
"Great. See you then."

I went back to the bathroom, toweled off and jumped into my clothes while I sang to Ada to calm her down. I was mopping up all of the water I had strewn through our condo when the buzzer sounded. It had been five minutes and he was here. Ada was fussing as I let him in. I grabbed her and introduced her as our family mascot. While she screamed, I showed him the closet.
"Oh, this isn't good. That's a problem. Is there a unit below you?" he asked.
"Nope. It's the basement." I replied.
"Okay. That's good. Can I see it?"

27

"Yep."

With Ada under my arm, I grabbed the key and headed downstairs.

"Oh, this is better than I thought. If you were on a higher floor this wouldn't work."

He proceeded to tell me how he could do it and quoted it out. I thanked him and we headed out of the basement. Again with Ada in my arms I fumbled with the MasterLock for a minute and finally got it to click, no thanks to him.

Back inside he checked out the closet again.

"I'll have to make a new hole in the wall since the electrical is in the way."

I laughed.

"What's so funny?"

"When the original plumber came to give us a quote, the electrician was here and I asked that question specifically and he told me it wouldn't be a problem. I work with engineers and married an architect so I understand the whole coordinating projects and tried to prevent this. Oh well. It's just drywall. Rick can fix that."

"Okay, so we'll cut the back wall open and put in a vent pipe at forty-eight inches."

"Sounds great." I replied.

He left and I called Rick to relay the message. We agreed to go ahead with the project.

After I called the plumber to give him the green light, I heard a strange thumping noise. I thought maybe it was cell phone interference with the computer speakers but they were turned off. After a few minutes I decided to investigate. Then it dawned on me. As I entered our bedroom I realized that I had tried to put Ada in her swing before I had set her in her bouncy seat. She didn't care for the swing so I folded it up and put it in our bedroom. I assumed the batteries were dead since it never seemed to swing on its own. To my surprise, there it was, folded up against the bedroom wall and rhythmically knocking against it. How about that. The batteries did work!

Now it was time for lunch. Ada nursed for a bit then went down for a mini nap. I heated up a baked potato. As soon as the microwave went off saying it was done, she woke up screaming.

"Hold on potato, I'll be back." I got her back to sleep long enough to reheat the potato, add cheese, bacon and just as I was adding the sour cream, she started screaming again. "Will I ever get to eat?" I put her back on the boob and ate with my magical mom skills (a.k.a. the mysterious third hand).

Moral of the story: Don't remodel, take showers when someone else is home, and always think twice before procreating.

Street Parking—Part One

If you live in the city and don't pay a bundle of money for a reserved parking space, I think you'll really relate to this. If you live in the burbs with a fancy driveway that fits four cars nicely, this will make you realize and be thankful for what you've got. And if you live on a farm where your entire front lawn can become a parking lot for an annual pig roast, well, just understand we're in two totally different places here.

Being a city dweller has its ups and downs. One upside is that we can park for free on the city streets—assuming we pay about $100 a year for a parking sticker and don't park in an illegal space or on the wrong side of the street during street cleaning days or within fifteen feet of a fire hydrant or within ten feet of a stop sign or... you get the point. One down side is actually being able to find a spot that your car will fit into, and having the parallel parking skills to squeeze into it without damaging anything.

You can imagine my excitement when I find an open space right in front of my condo, or even within ten car lengths. It's like winning the lotto. And if you move the car everyday and are lucky to do so when there is a lot of turnover on the street, you feel the lottery winner high most days. However, when you can't find a spot, life starts looking bad. Very bad, very quickly.

Having a child complicates this immensely. Before baby, if I was parked a block over, so what. Now if I'm a block over it's a question of "Can I carry her and the car seat that far without the stroller or do I have to make this a huge production?" "Can someone go get the car for me?" "Do we really need to run that errand today?"

Getting to the car isn't always the issue. If the car is right out front, my fear is giving up such a great spot and not being able to find one that is a similar distance from our home. When I get home I wonder "Will I be able to carry her, the car seat, and whatever we may have collected or purchased on our adventures back into the house with me?" And then I think, "Should I take the stroller with me just in case we don't find a good spot when we get back?" It's a lot to consider.

Last Friday I took Ada to see the doctor for the second cold of her life. She was three-months old mind you. I started the trip by asking the usual questions. The car was parked right across the street and I decided to chance getting a similar spot on the return so I didn't bother dragging the stroller out with me. We went to the doctor's office and returned an hour later to a complete lack of parking options. I drove around the block hoping something would open up as it usually did. No luck. I drove around again, and again, and again. Finally on the fifth time around our block, I pulled over to the side, put my hazard lights on and sat and waited for someone to pull out of a space in front of our house. When a car finally pulled out of a fifteen-minute loading zone, a car passing me had the nerve to consider pulling next to the space and tried to take it. Then he correctly realized I would kill him if he took the spot and that it was only a loading zone so he moved on. I didn't want the fifteen-minute spot either since I lived on this block and fifteen minutes just wouldn't cut it. I gave up and circled the block again. This time I noticed the woman in the car that was parked half in the fifteen-minute zone and half in the regular street parking area was about to move. I quickly lined up behind her and turned on my signal. She pulled out and I pulled in. I moved the car as far up as possible and rested against the bumper in front of me hoping that if the ticket guy saw that more than half of my car was in the regular street parking zone he wouldn't give me a ticket for the back half of my car in the loading zone.

I unloaded the baby, the car seat and the diaper bag and returned home through the outer and inner vestibule doors. I got the baby settled down for our afternoon routine and periodically peaked out the front window to see if I had been ticketed or if a fully legal space had opened up. After checking on the car ten times, I decided to risk it and just have my husband move it when he got home since I couldn't really move it without taking Ada in the car seat with me. It was almost worth getting a $50 ticket not to have to deal with all of this drama.

It was nearing the end of the day and I was waiting for my husband to get home. I put Ada in her crib and turned on her mobile so I could go wash my hands after changing her. Just out of curiosity I peaked out the front window. Oh my goodness! There was a spot! Right in front of the spot I was sort of in that was halfway legal! I had to make a decision. Should I do it? Quickly, I put my sandals on, grabbed the house keys, grabbed the car keys, thought to myself that the baby would be safe in her crib but I had to make this fast.

I whipped open the front door, the inner vestibule door, the outer vestibule door, ran down the three steps to the sidewalk, full out sprinted the twenty feet to the driver side door while I clicked the unlock button. I hopped in, turned on the ignition and pulled the car forward a whole eight feet! Yes! I got it. I put it in park, turned off the car, got out, pushed the lock button as I sprinted back to the building, up the two stairs, unlocked the outer vestibule door, then the inner vestibule door, then the front door and did my little happy dance. Ada was still cooing in her crib while she watched her mobile spin round and round. Woohoo!

Meanwhile, outside the people in traffic on my street were wondering why some crazy lady just sprinted out of her house and moved her car eight feet while in house slippers. After all, it was just a parking spot.

Moral of the story: Watch the Cubs game schedule when trying to park in front of my house on the first Friday in April, whenever in doubt, opt to take the stroller, and don't ever try to take a spot from a woman trying to park with a screaming baby in the back seat as it may very well cost you your life.

Street Parking—Part Two

Not only is it tough to find street parking in the city sometimes, often, okay frequently, but you rarely get the same spot. If you do, and it's a good spot, then you're having a super fantastic set of days and will be grinning from ear to ear for hours. For those of you who are a little more advanced in years, you know how hard it is to remember what you ate yesterday let alone where you parked the car. And parking the car in the city isn't like going to Walmart and parking the car and forgetting which aisle you finally decided on and how far down. No. Parking a car in the city involves knowing what street you parked it on, what side of the street, what block it's on, and if you need to have a special pass to park it there or move it by a certain time in the morning so you don't get a ticket. (And by ticket I mean a fifty dollar ticket. We're not talking the twenty-five cent fine you get for parking at the penny meters in my hometown of Sycamore. Fifty bucks a pop.)

And, I must add, living in the city also affords us the "luxury" of having only one car (meaning it is so expensive to live here and so tough to find a parking space that we can only afford one car and the pain it takes to park it.) So we share. That means that whenever we take the car somewhere, not only do we have to remember what street we parked it on, what block, what side and about how many cars in from the intersection it is, we also have to remember to tell our spouse where we parked it. Which leads me to this next story...

I have, quite possibly, the best husband in the world. (Many wives say it but I mean it, he really is awesome.) One night I was headed out to my knitting club with baby Ada in her car seat. I had fed her, bundled her up, packed her snugly into her car seat, and headed out to find the car. I called my wonderful husband and asked him where he parked the car since he had it last. He said he thought it was on Wellington, on our side of the street, half way or three quarters of the way down our block. "You think that's where it is or you know? It's two degrees out and I have the baby with me."
"I'm pretty sure," he replied with a sense of uncertainty.
"It better be."
"Yeah, it is. I think."

Still not convinced, I grabbed Ada in her car seat and my knitting basket (I was working on a baby blanket for her that I hoped to have done before she turned twenty.) I also had my hat, gloves, winter coat, winter boots, house keys, car keys, purse and cell phone. We were ready. We headed out our front door, shimmied through the inner vestibule door, then the outer vestibule door, and into the freezing cold night air that stole my breath and threatened to never give it back.

Down the sidewalk we went, making footprints in the newly fallen snow. Man this kid was heavy. She was about ten pounds and the car seat was probably another five and my super mom upper arm muscles hadn't come in yet. We were walking. Actually I was walking and leaning my upper body to the right to counteract the weight of the car seat as it scraped my left thigh while she slept in her cozy Bundle Me. I'd put my right glove in my pocket so I could hold the car keys and push the clicker so that if I got close to the car, the lights would flash. Most of you suburbanites just think those lights are for "security purposes" or to let you know the car is locked. Let me tell you. They are really handy when you are trying to figure out which Honda Civic is yours when it's one of the most popular cars in the city and all of the cars are covered in snow. Oh, and for fun, add in the fact that you don't know where you, or your spouse in this case, parked the car.

So, yes, I walked down the street, pushing the button as I went. My exposed hand was frozen. I got to the other end of our street without seeing our car. I started back toward the house continuing to click the button. Nothing. I dug out my cell phone and called my fabulous husband at work.
Sternly I said, "Rick. Where is the car?"
"I told you it's on Wellington."
"Where exactly on Wellington?"
"Well, I can't remember."
"I'm freezing, carrying the baby in the car seat and this is not the time for you to not be sure about where you parked the car."
"It could be across the street."
"It could be? Or it is?"
"I think it is."

Click. I hung up. I walked across the street as I tried to take a deep breath. A kind elderly woman pushing a cart on wheels—the kind you take to the grocery store when you live in the city and want to save your wrists from breaking if you were to lug it all back home—asked me if she could help me as I was obviously frustrated. I thanked her kindly and explained that my husband lost our car. She asked me if I'd like to put the car seat on her cart if we were going the same way. I explained that I was actually going the other way but thanked her profusely as

I dialed my husband's number again.

"Rick." The anger in my voice was increasing. "Where is the @#%^% car?"
"I told you, it's across the street."
"No, it isn't. I've been up and down our block two and a half times now. Where is the #$^^%@ car already?" I asked curtly, my frozen fingers throbbing as I grasped the cell phone and refrained from whipping it at the snowy sidewalk and throwing the tantrum of the century.
"It's not on our block. Across the street to the West, meaning on Wellington but past Clark Street."
"Are you kidding me?"
"That's what I said the first time. Across the street."
"I thought you meant the North side of Wellington. Forget it."

Disheartened, and really, really, really mad at this point, I hung up on him again, re-crossed our street and headed toward Clark Street. By now, my biceps were screaming, my fingers were entering the early stages of frost bite, and I had to wait for the light to change green to give me a walk signal. After what seemed like hours, I got the little white man walk signal and awkwardly waddled across the street alternating the car seat from my left side to my right side and back again.

As if this wasn't enough of a challenge, it was rush hour and a load of passengers had just gotten off the El and were coming toward me. While dodging the onslaught of commuters and their duffel bags, mongo purses, briefcases and puffy coats, I retrieved the keys from my pocket and continued pushing the unlock button. My hand felt like it might fall off at this point. I was four cars in when finally the lights flickered from under the snow. Thank goodness! I found it. Fumbling with my glove and my keys in my right hand, I made my final approach to the passenger side of the car. I swung the car seat around next to the back door and... where were my keys? I just had them. That was how I knew this was my car. I checked my pocket. Nope. The folds of Ada's Bundle Me? No. The snow next to the car? No. My eyes were starting to well up and I felt an emotional breakdown coming on. I looked up and glanced to my right when an Asian woman approached me and said "Are these your keys?"
"Yes!" I replied and thanked her profusely. I must have dropped them when my hand went numb from the cold.

Quickly, for fear of losing my entire limb instead of just my hand, I unlocked the car, loaded Ada inside, started the engine, turned on the defrost and grabbed the snow scraper. Just then, my phone rang. It was the two knitting ladies calling to check on me since I was supposed to be downtown to pick them up five minutes ago. "I caught a bit of a snag. I'll pick up my husband, throw him in the river and be right there to get you guys."

With a few quick sweeps of the snow brush, the car was cleaned and we were on our way to get my husband from work. We picked him up and I chose the silent route. He looked me in the eyes and said, "Sorry". We then proceeded to get my knitting buddies from their office, arrived at knitting and fittingly sent my husband away with the car since there was nowhere to park nearby my friend's South Loop apartment.

Moral of the story: Even the best husband in the world has his bad days, winter in Chicago can be really, really, really cold, and foregoing a reserved parking spot may save you money but not your marriage, strike that, I mean sanity.

To Baby, or Not to Baby

This is a huge slap across the face to anyone you've ever known who thinks having a baby will SAVE their marriage. Hello! Wake up people. This comes to me in light of hearing a newly divorced gentlemen say "I think we'd still be together if we had kids." And from having friends and relatives say "I was trying to get pregnant right before we split up to save the marriage." WHAT??? Can someone explain to me how that's supposed to work?

A strong marriage takes work. It's a full-time job. So is having a job. And having a baby is the equivalent of three full-time jobs. So how does that add up?

I must say that I am amazed on a daily basis as to how single mothers, teenagers, women here from foreign countries without family to help them out, and low income families do it. As I ask this question over and over, everyone keeps telling me "You do what you've got to do."

Don't get me wrong here. Being a parent is the coolest thing ever, but it is the hardest job I've ever had. I feel so blessed to have a strong marriage, family within two hours from us and able to help out, friends willing to babysit and tolerate our screaming baby at brunch on Sundays. I'm also thankful to have found a few local mom groups that have been a great resource for answering the everyday questions that a new mom faces.

So what about the job of parent appeals to people in a relationship crisis? I want to know if there is some sort of biological reason that this happens to people because I can't figure it out. Do people just think babies come out like a little cupid shooting love darts at everyone they see and magically repairing marriages and relationships?

And if I happen to be hitting too close to home for anyone... can someone please explain why this happens? Why did you do it? What motivates someone to want to bring a child into a crap relationship voluntarily? Or do they not even consider the consequences and just hope that a baby will wash away their failures and make everything better? If you aren't in love anymore—will a baby change that? If you fight about money and finances to begin with, as most couples do, it surely won't help since, NEWS FLASH, this just in... babies are expensive.

The only thing I can think of is that a baby would cause a distraction long enough to maybe iron out your differences. But chances of that working are slim and short lived. Babies can live to be one hundred these days. Would it be worth it to be connected to a bad relationship for the rest of your life? I think not. But bless those who do get pregnant before they have a chance to read this or get talked out of it by a good friend.

Moral of the story: Pregnancy does not a relationship save.

Laundry, Remodeling, & Relatives

I mentioned babies soil things quickly so you do a lot of laundry as a mom. Hence the reason we decided to add a washer/dryer to our bedroom closet.

I must say that the thing is frigging AWESOME... But it was insanely disruptive to remodel. Having a small home to begin with, space was important to us. We lived out of the baby's closet for two months. Oh yes, this process took two months. My fabulous husband gave up several weekends of his time, hours that could have been spent playing with the baby, and he even slept on the living room floor for a week so I could have the couch as we waited to clean our drywall-dust-covered bedroom. It was not easy.

A huge "Thanks" went out to our families and friends for all of their help during this crazy time. Our friends from back home came to demo the wall, my brother-in-law and his girlfriend came the day I got diagnosed with strep throat to help re-drywall and babysit, my mother came to help clean and bring some sense of order to the house, and my fantastic friends came to entertain me, fold laundry, babysit, and just hang out without freaking out about the fact that my home looked like it was recently ransacked by a wild boar. Rick's parents came in to help us re-assemble our home. And I enjoyed getting our lives back to normal.

It wasn't the best week to do this since I was recovering from strep throat, the baby had a sinus infection and we had chosen this week to try the "cry it out" method—which I might add was working very well. I was getting a good deal of sleep, for which I was very thankful, but I also decided that this was the week that my maternity leave was officially over and I launched my own marketing consulting firm. I was hoping to have my first client on board in a week or so and I was actively seeking additional clients.

At least my schedule was easy as far as appointments went. Ada was doing well in daycare and between walks with neighbors and the fact that I had a sixteen-and-a-half pound four-month old, I got quite a good workout without even trying.

Moral of the story: Build a strong network of friends and family to help you through all that gets thrown your way, avoid remodeling, and try not to bite off more that you can chew as you only live for so long.

Never Enough Momma Clothes

As a new mom, I quickly learned what everyone means by saying that "You can never have too many baby clothes." With the way we had to do laundry, that was surely the case. However, they typically failed to mention that I could never have too many mommy or daddy clothes either.

When I heard "Babies spit up, it's normal". I didn't really associate that with it being all over me and her dad all the time. And I mean ALL of the time. I had this running joke with daycare that we were going to statistically prove that Ada threw up on me more than any other mother (as in every time I picked her up at the end of the day). I never went home with a clean shoulder. And it wouldn't have been so bad but for the laundry. The first time she threw up on me at daycare, I was wearing a black jacket that had a thin layer of quilted stuffing to provide a little warmth. She goobered on my shoulder and I thought nothing of it, wiped it off and went on my merry way. The next day I picked my husband up from work and ran to the grocery store before picking Ada up from daycare. The weather was still a bit chilly so I put on my black jacket. Everything was fine until I got into the car and turned on the heat a bit. By the time I got to his office I had the windows down and was trying to keep myself from puking. Being that the spit up was on my shoulder and a day old, it was right in my face and stinky. Every time I looked over to talk to my husband, the smell would overwhelm me and I would start to gag. Needless to say, we made that trip to the store and daycare as short as possible. And when we got to daycare, she threw up on the other shoulder—of course.

The next week, since my black coat was in the laundry and the weather was a bit warmer, I decided to wear a teal rain coat. Again, throw up on my shoulder. The following day, I opted to go coatless. I thought I could trick her into not throwing up on my coat since I wasn't wearing one. Unfortunately I was wearing one of my favorite t-shirts from Threadless. It had a refrigerator running on it. Somehow I had forgotten that the stats for that t-shirt were even worse than for my coats. She threw up on it on the way home from Easter—about half-an-hour in during a five-hour car ride. That was pleasant. And she had thrown up on it four other times in the four weeks that I had owned it. My husband had even taken the time to pre-treat the stains in an attempt to get the goober remnants to go away, with some luck, knowing that this was my new favorite shirt.

So there I was, at daycare, holding Ada while wearing my favorite t-shirt and of course, she threw up. Not only on my shoulder that time. That time she managed to get my shoulder and created a spit-up river down the front of my entire shirt. As I just chuckled, one of the daycare assistants tried to wipe it off with a burp cloth and finally just handed it to me since my entire left boob was covered in regurgitated breast milk. Nice. Somehow I was going to have to teach Ada that I didn't want the breast milk back. At all. Ever. Not on my coat, not on my refrigerator, not on my floor, not on my front door. Not with a hat or a cat, or a cat in a hat, or any other shape or form. I don't want it back.

Moral of the story: Babies really do spit up a lot, you can NEVER have enough burp cloths when you need them, and it might be smart to travel with a backup mommy and daddy outfit too.

Baby Clothes

To all of you who love to shop for baby clothes, here are a few
practical tips from a mom.
Try to get things on sale or clearance since:
1) you don't know how long it will last
2) babies stain things
3) you can buy more for the same amount of money
4) the baby might not even fit into it during the season it is
made for

Don't buy clothes with buttons, snaps or other decorative stuff
(i.e. crap) up the back because baby spends most of her time
laying on her back and that would not be comfy—do unto
babies as you would have done unto you. Which leads me to my
next point...

Get the kid some pants. I have a million Onesies and three pair
of pants, none of them that match more than one Onesie. I
default to one pair of pants all the time, which rarely match and
frequently are in the wash. And baby's legs get cold.

Outfits that zip from heal to chin with footies are awesome.
They may not be the most fashionable thing out there but if
mom or dad is taking baby to the doctor, this is the outfit of
choice. The doctor's office makes you undress the baby, re-
dress the baby, and you may have to change the baby again
while you're there so it just makes life easier for everyone.
Especially when they are crying after getting their vaccines.

Pajamas with the hand covers for baby's first few weeks and
months are great. Her fingernails are sharp and it makes Mom
feel awful when she notices Baby has a giant mark of Zorro (or
the Harry Potter lightening bolt for generation Y-ers) on her
forehead from a stray fingernail gone wild in the middle of the
night.

The soft and fluffy fleece blankets from Target that are 100%
polyester suck. Don't waste your time with them because they
pill up like crazy in the wash and quickly become the crappiest
blanket on the block. Not cool.

Sunhats and sunglasses often get overlooked on the baby

shower list but would come in really handy—even in winter. And so would music for baby—but I digress as that is a whole different entry. A mom can never have enough burp cloths, wash cloths, baby socks and, believe it or not, baby blankets.

And if a mom has decided on cloth diapers, she'll need clothes with extra length in the torso as the diaper takes up a bit more room. When in doubt, buy bigger as babies tend to grow into things and the sizing on most baby clothes completely lies.

Moral of the story: Shopping for baby is tougher than it appears, look for ease of dressing and undressing in addition to cuteness, and avoid crappy fleece blankets so your gifts don't suck.

For Crying out Loud!

There are many different theories on sleep training and what method to use, who is the current expert, blah bitti blah blah. My husband and I finally decided to go to the dark side and try the "cry it out" method. Note: This is not for everyone and I don't want a hundred parents telling me I'm a bad mother. Our decision was made out of a moment of weakness and frustration. And it is one of the hardest things we've ever had to do. I gladly admit as of a few months ago I was firmly on the "No way am I going to make my kid cry it out. That's insane. There has to be a better way," bandwagon, but we haven't found a better way.

For a little bit of background, my friend Anne has a sister, Rachel, who has two adorable kids. While I was pregnant, I babysat for Rachel and found it to be the easiest gig I've ever had. I went to her house and Rachel explained that her maybe ten-month-old (mommy brain fails me) daughter went to bed at seven and her two-year-old son at eight. To put her daughter to bed, I just changed her diaper, put on her pajamas, read her two books, set her in the crib, turned off the light, shut the door and walked away to go play games with her son. Too easy. To put her son to bed was a bit more difficult because I didn't speak two-year old. I changed his diaper, got him into pajamas, he brushed his teeth, and we read two books. Then he got into his crib and kept saying something like "I love knuckles". After about five minutes of him pointing, me feeling like the dumbest person on earth and handing him every toy in his room only to be told "No" as he shook his head and repeated "I love knuckles", I finally figured it out. He had this routine every night where he and his parents said "I love you", they hugged, and then they knocked knuckles (totally a guy thing—hence my complete lack of comprehension). Once I figured that out, he zipped up his crib cover (which prevented him from falling out as it is a dome-like tent) and I headed out the door. But I was called back to rescue him as I forgot to close the blinds. So I adjusted the blinds and again shut the door. I was done. It was eight fifteen at night and I was done babysitting. No crying. No fussing. Nada. It was awesome! These were the perfect kids!

So the other night, my friend Anne was over for dinner and it was time to put Ada to bed. Rick and I had been doing the "feed her to sleep and hope that she doesn't wake up as we transfer her to the crib" method. And sometimes the "bounce her on my knee until she goes cross-eyed and passes out" method. And frequently the "rock the baby in your arms for an hour while bouncing up and down and swaying back and forth while saying 'Shhhh' and praying that your arms/back/hips don't give out" method. After several nights of exhaustion and a deep desire to spend more than five minutes of adult time with my husband, we were looking to try anything else. Anne suggested we try the "cry it out" method. She said it worked for her sister Rachel in about two days and the kids have been great ever since. "So that's her trick." I said. Hmmm. It sounded too good to be true. The theory was that we would listen to Ada cry for half an hour, two nights or so, then just lay her in the crib and she'd be trained to fall asleep on her own. Instantly we jumped on the idea. And thankfully Anne volunteered to sit and distract me while Ada cried for twenty-five minutes that night. It was tough but I did my best to stay strong and knew that the result would be way better for us both in the end. I'm not saying it was easy by any means. But I'm still alive and that was a week ago.

At daycare on Wednesday they let her "cry it out" for forty-five minutes and that was tough to take as a mom. I could just imagine my poor little Ada screaming for that long and it hurt. But at least she took a good nap at daycare since napping had been a bit of a struggle.

On Friday I mentioned to my friends at Mom Network that I was trying the "cry it out" method and it was working pretty well. I got a few weird looks and some comments about how it isn't for everyone, some babies don't deal with it well and freak out, and the long term effects of it haven't been studied. All of which made me doubt myself a bit and turned me into a bit of a psycho mom about it.

Now I'd be a complete liar if I said this was the best thing to do for every child and every mother. And I'd be lying if I said I didn't have a complete break down on Saturday while Rick was out running errands as I tried to get her to take a morning nap and she cried for what seemed like forty-five minutes. But the result of her long crying stint and my long crying stint actually was a really good thing too. Rick came home early from running errands and we got to talk about how things were going and what we could do to make things run a little more smoothly. He also told me to stop doubting myself as a parent because I am doing a good job and this isn't going to scar her for life (take note men, supporting your wife is SO important and helpful and the number one cause for her not to completely go insane on you).

From our little talk on Saturday we decided to be consistent and be sure to always ask "Why?" whenever Ada was crying. Was she wet? Hungry? Gassy? Tired? And we identified the types of cries she has. As the five cries a baby makes were featured on Oprah, "Neh" means hungry. If she was wet or dirty her diaper would be the proof. If she was gassy, we might not know unless we listened for a fart, burped her, or pushed her legs up to her chest and tried to wiggle something loose. And if she was tired, we needed to watch for the signs. For Ada, rubbing her eyes, yawning, and a screaming a miserable whining cry meant we were too late. She was overtired. But slowing down, losing focus, getting cuddly were all ways she was trying to say "Hey, I need a nap!" Once we figured all of that out, we settled into a routine of some sort. I watched for the signals, fed her, changed her diaper and then laid her down with a kiss and shut the door to her room. Within minutes, she was done crying and fast asleep. The time she spent crying was less and less each time. And I learned to take a shower, go to the back of the house, or call Rick while she cried. Her little voice tended to go in waves and the quiet between the crying waves lengthened until eventually she was out cold. A beautiful thing.

Again, it isn't for everyone. But if you want to learn more you can try to read this book by Dr. Marc Weissbluth called *Healthy Sleep Habits, Happy Child*. At times the book is way too detailed but I think there are some good things to get out of it, too.

Moral of the story: Don't doubt your skills as a mother, do what you feel is right for your child, and most important of all be consistent in whatever you do.

Cloth Diapers Note

You really do need to wash your cloth diapers four or five times before you use them to get them to be absorbent. It doesn't really make sense to me why but Rick and I forgot to wash the next size up that we have and started using them after about one or two washes. Boy, were we in for it. Ada leaked all over the place because the pee just pooled on the diaper. Now that we've washed them, all is well with the world again.

And you do have to get used to folding the diapers and finagling them into the covers. It might take a little extra time but is well worth the effort.

Moral of the story: Good luck to those other parents who join forces with me in saving the world one cloth diaper at a time. It is not easy.

Can't Anybody Just Agree?

Yet another thing I've learned in motherhood is that none of the "experts" can agree on anything. It's kind of like marketing in the way that we marketers can find a way to use the research to prove whatever outcome is in our favor. "Pediatrician Recommended" might mean that a company paid a pediatrician $100 to say sure, use that lotion. But for some reason, the public believes that if a pediatrician recommended it, it must be good. Who cares if the pediatrician is ninety years old, an alcoholic, and has never even seen the product he is recommending. You just have to use some common sense and your best judgment.

With that said, here are a few things I've found that articles, doctors and mothers can't agree on and the stance I've taken on them. Maybe it will help save someone the trouble of trying to find the so-called right answer since it doesn't exist. Caution: This is probably way too much information for some people (i.e. queasy men) so proceed with caution.

Can you eat peanut butter while breastfeeding or not? My answer: Nobody knows. If you don't have allergies in your family, eat the friggin' peanut butter. If you are worried about it, don't. I personally don't think that the small quantities of peanut butter I eat are going to cause Ada to have peanut allergies. I've read studies that support both sides. I put peanut butter on my pancakes this morning and will deal with the consequences.

I do, however, think that you should avoid giving babies honey for their first year because it can cause botulism which can be deadly. And I don't need honey that badly.

Breastfeeding moms should avoid using birth control with estrogen because it will lower the mother's milk supply. My answer: I have recently read mixed reports on this. Most doctors seem to prescribe the mini pill which has no estrogen. That's great but after a few months it can cause depression, it isn't as effective as other methods, you have to take the pill within three hours of the same time everyday or it loses its effectiveness, among other issues. I've recently been told and read that the patch and NuvaRing can be used since they don't deliver the estrogen via pill so they don't affect the milk supply as much if at all. My totally worthless and absolutely unprofessional opinion is to use condoms for the first few months until you get the whole breastfeeding thing under control and you have stockpiled some milk. Then give something else a try if you feel like it.

Breastfeeding will prevent you from getting pregnant. My answer: Not true all the time. It will reduce the chances of you getting pregnant but it isn't an effective means of birth control. I know two people who have gotten pregnant while nursing. One intentionally, one unintentionally after her Dr. said she wouldn't get pregnant. One of the not so widely known benefits of nursing is that you don't necessarily get your period back for a few months, or even years for some people. I guess that isn't a benefit if you are trying to figure out when you might be ovulating though.

Is there such a thing as nipple confusion? My answer: Maybe in the very beginning. Try to just use the boob to feed your baby in the beginning if she has trouble latching on. Once she gets the hang of it, switch between boob and bottle, and have different people feed the baby from the bottle, including Mom. My doctor freaked out that I was feeding her with the bottle and breastfeeding but I've found that it doesn't make any difference. And try different bottles to see what works for the baby.

For all of you pregnant women, some doctors still recommend episiotomies. My answer: Don't let them do it. Studies show that it is better to tear instead of have the Dr. make a cut for vaginal births. Again I'm no expert but my Dr. said she won't do them unless things get really crazy and that is the only option. The theory is that your body will only tear as much as it needs to and where it needs to but a Dr. might cut more than you need and it would take longer to heal.

Once you have the baby, some doctors will say to clean the area around the umbilical cord with an alcohol wipe. My answer: It will fall off if you do so or not. Babies born in other countries survive just fine without alcohol wipes so do whatever you feel like. It really doesn't make a difference in my opinion.

Should you give your baby water? My answer: I don't know but a tiny bit probably won't hurt. A dietitian told me yes. Give them a little water so that they get used to it but never more than an ounce or two since they will fill their tiny tummies with water and not get the nutrients they need from their milk. My doctor recommends that I don't give her water as she gets plenty from my milk. I don't think an ounce here or there will hurt her as long as you pay attention to the fluoride content so you don't mess up her teeth (even before they come in the fluoride can damage them.) And be sure that she is getting enough milk.

Are gas drops like Mylacon okay for babies? My answer: Heck yeah. They are a lifesaver. Some people think they haven't been proven to work. Some think they are fine. Ada loves them and they do seem to help relieve her gas. But they have also been proven to be just as effective as a placebo so it might be all in my head.

Do babies get sinus infections? My answer: I don't know for sure since I've had two doctors tell me opposite answers but Ada had green snot coming out of her nose like mad and we put her on Amoxicillin and now it is much better. So I'm assuming babies' sinuses develop sometime around four months since that's when the snot appeared. Don't rule it out I guess is what I'm saying and if baby has green snot, do something about it.

Should I vaccinate my baby? Will it cause autism? My answer: I do believe in vaccinating your children because the benefits strongly outweigh the risks. The whole issue of autism is something that I'm not sure anyone understands. It seems to be related to diet on some level. There is one ingredient in certain vaccines that people think causes it. I'm not sure what that ingredient is, but educate yourself and try to avoid vaccines that have that ingredient. Talk to your doctor and learn more about it. I just heard about a family (on Oprah's Big Give) that has five children who are all on the autism spectrum. That makes me think it is genetic, or environmental, but I'm a marketing major with an MBA.

I'm not a doctor or a specialist in this stuff. These are my best guesses on how to parent my kid. Take them or leave them but at least pay attention and educate yourself.

Moral of the story: Try to make educated decisions as best you can when it comes to parenting. Your doctor probably doesn't know everything there is to know about babies and the Universe so feel free to double check or get a second opinion and question what they say. And follow your gut because intuition is too powerful to ignore.

The Art of Pumping

For those of you who don't know much about nursing, it seems to have changed quite a bit since my mom's generation experienced it. Back in the day (when my parents were walking to school uphill both ways barefoot in the snow as the story goes) they didn't have electric breast pumps, and probably not even electricity—okay, just kidding about that part—but they had to pump manually. And breastfeeding wasn't encouraged back then because someone decided (probably someone in marketing no less) that formula was better for babies. The list of benefits from nursing is quite impressive and includes passing antibodies from mom to baby to help boost baby's immune system. It is also a great way to bond and gives you a major advantage over dad since he can't compete with your huge knockers. He can just envy them and dream of getting a turn someday.

Now, of course, times have changed and I've heard there is actually a law that gives every infant the right to breast milk. There are breast milk donors and breast milk banks even. With the increase in the popularity of nursing and society slowly starting to accept public breastfeeding, I decided I'd give it a try. And I'm not sure how many of you have seen the price for a can of formula these days, but nursing your baby saves some serious cash.

Knowing the difference in how breastfeeding was perceived from when I was born to today, you can imagine my mom's surprise when I arrived home from the hospital and ran around topless for a few days. After having just been through labor, all concerns for privacy were out the window and I really didn't care who saw me naked. And when you first try to breastfeed you realize that it isn't easy and it isn't for everyone. Some people have an easier time of it. Some babies just don't want to cooperate. I was lucky that it came easily to me and Ada took to it right away. But it was still very painful in the beginning and tearful at times, as you can probably imagine.

For those of you considering nursing, I highly recommend you give it a try and request a consultation with a lactation consultant while you're at the hospital. They can really help get you started. There is also a book called *The Nursing Mother's Companion: Revised Edition* that is a good reference. And be sure to have some Medela Tender Care Lanolin on hand for when your nipples get sore. The truth hurts and so do your nipples for the first few weeks. But if you can get the baby to latch on correctly from the get go, you'll have a much better chance of lasting through those painful times. The first week is the most important as that is when your body produces "liquid gold" which is colostrum - a thicker milk that has all the yummy good stuff baby needs to stay healthy. And if you can make it through the first month, you're in the clear for the most part. But be sure to ask for help and get the number of someone who has done it or your local La Leche group or a breastfeeding consultant because you need someone to cry to when the going gets rough.

And just remember, it does get better (for most people, not everyone). By three or four months the pain is gone and you can't wait for baby to feed because you're bursting with milk and need the release.

As far as milk production goes, my mother was again surprised that contrary to popular belief, little boobs can produce as much as big boobs and for once in our lifetime, size doesn't really matter. Unless you're my husband who just thinks breastfeeding is the coolest since I am frequently flashing boob around the house and I've increased a few cup sizes along the way. Lucky guy.

As for my single friends, who come to hang out at my house and get a glimpse of baby Ada, I've shocked most of them as I either latch Ada on a boob or have to pump when she's asleep. I try to be respectful and not flash too much skin but sometimes that is easier said than done. I know I have amazed many a friend while pumping since it is such a foreign concept for most. One night at knitting club I hooked up my pump and was quickly compared to a milk cow. The pumping action intrigued some while freaking the crap out of others. It can support the argument for birth control too since being milked isn't high on one's list of things to do in life.

And many a friend, and even cousin Ted, have noted that the rhythmic noise the pump makes sounds like the pump is saying something. I mostly hear "find a penny, find a penny". But it says something different to everyone. Cousin Ted heard something more like "gotta pee, gotta pee". I guess it all depends on what you're concerned about subconsciously.

So the whole point of this entry, the Art of Pumping is just that. An art. Many of my friends have been amazed at how much I can accomplish while pumping but what they don't realize is that I have found this nifty little gadget that makes my pump hands-free. An Easy Expression Hands Free Bustier Nursing Bra. It is a tube top with a zipper up the front and a hole cut out for each nipple. (Sexy, I know. Austin Powers would be envious. Yeah, baby!) This gadget holds the "funnels", as I call them, to your chest so that you don't have to. It is quite comfortable and really adds to my productivity. Just this week I amazed myself by pumping in the bathroom while putting on my make-up. It was a lot easier than I though and has taken multi-tasking to a whole new level.

We'll see how this art form continues as I face two new challenges. One is Ada getting teeth and how that will affect my comfort level in the coming months. The other being a need to pump while out and about in the city while Ada is at daycare. Supposedly Nordstroms on Michigan Ave has a mommy room I can use to pump if I'm ever in that area. I've only had to pump while out and about once thus far and I did so before getting a one hour massage so they gave me access to the massage room beforehand. I can only imagine how difficult it can be for working mothers who don't have facilities specifically for nursing. I know firsthand how frustrating and disgusting it is to nurse Ada while standing in a dingy bathroom that is anything but mom-friendly. Inhaling the smell of the nasty bathroom air freshener with every breath as you try not to touch any cootie-covered surfaces is not pleasant. All while averting your eyes from focusing on the partial toilet seat and hoping your back doesn't give out as you stand holding your rapidly growing child in your arms for anywhere from ten minutes to an hour as the little one drinks from the fountain of mom.

Moral of the story: Nursing is a great experience that is not for everyone, plan ahead to find nursing-friendly locations when you are out and about, and splurge on the hands-free gadget or make one of your own as it really is a fabulous thing.

First Impressions

This week I was blessed to have my good friend Cadence come visit to meet our little angel. Unfortunately for everyone, our little angel wasn't feeling her best and decided to show Cadence her more devilish side. She got her four-month shots on Monday and spent Cadence's Wednesday and Thursday visit being a fussy mess. She was at daycare both days which left little time to make the ever important first impression. Lucky for all of us, she was in bed at seven and their meeting was kept short. During that small window of time, however, Ada was able to show off her amazing ability to throw up on Mommy at every opportunity. She also displayed her vocal talents by practicing a wide variety of screams, some during the middle of the night as she put on a waterworks show from her diaper that even the Bellagio couldn't compete with. And she couldn't pass up an opportunity to let Cadence know she has the fortitude and lung capacity to make sure the entire North Side of the city of Chicago is aware that she has arrived. Hopefully Auntie Cadence will be overwhelmed by Ada's adorableness, forget all the drama of the weekend, and return again soon. Maybe I should have given her a few more Killer Margaritas from Cesar's. Better luck next time baby.

Moral of the story: You do not have any control over how your infant will act so prepare to apologize often for her behavior.

Fascination with Fans?

Why is it that babies love ceiling fans so much? Either on or off, Ada never seems to get tired of the ceiling fan. This weekend, while napping on Granny and Grandpa's bed, she awoke and just lay there staring at the fan. Round and round. If it weren't for me peeking in to check on her and noticing the newest member of the family—Sadie the one-year-old beagle who joined Aunt Terri's family one day prior—circling Ada on the bed, she may have stared at the fan while I enjoyed my lunch. But most moms know, if your food is hot, the baby is fussy.

Moral of the story: "Get it while it's hot" means eating a meal while it still harbors some warmth from the kitchen. Oh, and get a ceiling fan to bring joy into your child's life.

May

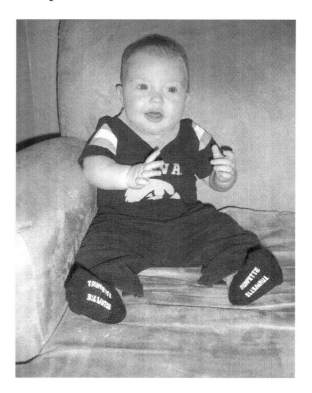

Kid Comparisons

I have to say that I am quite happy that my doctor wasn't comparing my kid to the "average" every time I went in to see her. (Let me digress briefly to say—why is it that whenever I say "I took Ada to the doctor…" most people respond with "What did HE say?" Even the nurse on the Nurse Advice line I called one day assumed she was a he. I happen to have all female doctors that I go to and think they are all great. I think it is partly because we don't have a female version of doctor like we do for waiter or waitress. Maybe I'll invent doctoress but what would the abbreviation for Dr. be? Dres.?) Okay, back on track. So, not comparing my kid to the average…. I've been in to see the doctoress a lot since Ada was born—probably ten times, which seems like a lot to me. I mean, as adults we only go in once or twice a year if we are fairly healthy and this little munchkin is only four-months old. Babies go in for a one-week checkup, one-month checkup, two-month shots, four-month shots, and several more I'm not sure when. But the average— there is that word again—baby gets ten colds a year. I've already taken her in about four times for being sick and treated her for a sinus infection. I think she is on cold number three— and that's a lot of snot and boogers so be prepared all of you not-yet-parents.

Where was I? Average. At four months, Rick and I were amazed that our baby who started out at eight pounds was now sixteen pounds, eight ounces. I knew she would double her weight in the first six months but the first four months seemed ahead of schedule. I asked, "Where is Ada on the national chart of averages?"
 To which my female doctor replied, "She's off the chart for weight, and over the ninety-fifth percentile for height."
What? I have a big baby! Is that a good thing or a bad thing? She told me not to worry as things will even out as she gets older. She's just front loading all of her growth spurts. Okay...

I asked my neighbor who has baby Eva how much Eva weighs and her stats. Same as Ada. Yeah! We both have crazy big babies that are off the charts. Woohoo! We aren't alone. But going out in public is a whole different story. "Wow! What a big baby!" is the new standard comment.
"Yeah, she's eating well and growing fast." I reply.
Or "How old is she?" (Sometimes they say HE even if she's wearing light pink—go figure.)
"She's four months."
"Wow. My eight-month old is smaller than her."
To which I think, "Holy crap what have I done to this child?" It used to be that everyone commented on how cute she was and what beautiful blue eyes she had but now they have switched to how quickly she has grown. I don't have much to compare her to but baby Eva next door and they are similar so I'm not worried. It's just weird when she came back from daycare in Claire's clothes that fit Ada nicely (I forgot to send a backup outfit one day and that's all they had to put her in after a blowout) and they told me Claire is nine-months old and wears the same size as Ada. And daycare workers would know if she is big on average since they see several kids her age daily.

The good news about having a big baby is that they tend to sleep through the night sooner since their bodies need to be a certain weight before they can physically sleep that long without needing to eat. The studies say twelve pounds/twelve-weeks old or fourteen pounds/fourteen-weeks old is when they are able to make it through the night. We hit that milestone early. (For which I am very thankful.)

The bad news is that I don't want to give her a complex about her size. At Mom Network I was told that studies show that whatever you tell your kids at age four is what they will be. If you say they are lazy, they will be lazy for the rest of their lives. So at least I have some time to re-train myself. But I can't help but catch myself every time I say, "Look at your cute Budda belly," or when I call her "pumpkin". I can't say, "You're my big girl," either since it is okay to say that to little boys but not little girls. Again with the gender crap.

I'm trying to call her my "little monkey" instead just so that it isn't related to anything big and round. And her daycare is calling her "cupcake" since she has a cupcake outfit. I thought about "muffin" but then I thought of muffin tops being the flab hanging over the waist of a pair of jeans and, well, that just isn't working for me either. It's not like she'll have any trouble with her weight growing up as both my husband and I have insanely high metabolisms and have to really work hard to put on any weight, but still. If she is above average for height and weight, she might be teased and called "Amazon Woman" by her peers. I guess I just have to tell Eva's mom that they can never move because Eva and Ada have to stick together in their bigness. They can be the twin towers—but see that doesn't even work since 9/11.

I guess I'll just hope that she doesn't turn into a bully and use her size to intimidate other kids, unless it's on the soccer field or basketball court or wherever else intimidation is socially acceptable. And it could be worse. She could be below average. I'll take what I got and know that there is just more of her to love and cuddle with. And I'll pray that she doesn't decide to join the WWF (World Wrestling Federation not World Wildlife Foundation).

Moral of the story: It's okay to be above average (half of us always are if you think about it), it is important to love your child for who they are, and it is best not to make a big deal when people compare your child to theirs knowing that they all develop differently—and that's okay.

Who Knew Teeth Are Such a Pain?

Now I understand why the dentist harps on us all to brush and floss and visit him/her (again with the Dentist gender thing too—Dentistess?) regularly. Poor little Ada is having a heck of a time teething. Finally today I broke down and gave her some baby Motrin. The Tylenol isn't cutting it (no pun intended), and the Orajel is only working so well. I have found one trick to stop her screaming though. I put her in the Baby Bjorn and go for a walk. And walk. And walk some more. I'm at the point where I want to borrow my neighbor's dog just so I feel that we have a purpose or sense of direction. Today we had to go to the post office and it was a great reason to get out of the house. But I'm not one to just go on a walk. Typically I go with a friend or have a mission. That's one of the amazing things I'm learning about having a daughter. She's making me slow down, pay attention to her and only her, and enjoy some free time for myself. (Unless Rick and I are trying to sit down for a meal in which case I'm learning to eat faster than humanly possible, re-heat everything, eat after my meal is cold, or eat one-handed while bouncing her on my knee or feeding her a bottle.)

I will say that I am very thankful she decided to start teething while the weather is nice. I can't complain about being forced to go on walks when it is sunny and seventy and the flowers are in full bloom. It's not all that bad. And she has so much to distract her from the pain of her teeth that she just hangs out and quietly enjoys everything she sees. Today we sat on a bench in front of the local ice cream shop and just watched the people go by. It's always fun when they say hi or walk by with other infants and the babies check each other out.

Moral of the story: Try to find the good things when the going gets rough, get creative with ways to distract children from pain, and when nothing else works take a few deep breaths and count to ten slowly.

Crib Sheets Make Me Cry

I understand that Sudden Infant Death Syndrome (SIDS) is very dangerous and researchers haven't figured it out yet, yada yada. I get that baby needs to sleep on her back and suck a pacifier if she'll take one so that she can breath easily and have less of a chance of suffocation. It even makes sense that you wait to use the crib bumpers, pillows and stuffed animals in the crib. (Which is why it baffles me that they even sell crib bumpers since we aren't supposed to use them.) But is it really necessary to make the dang crib sheets so tight that I can't get them on? Seriously? I dread any time Ada soils her crib sheet because I am barely strong enough to change it. And I'm not patient so that doesn't help either. (This is why my husband makes our bed too. I hate doing it.)

Yesterday morning, Ada leaked on her sheet a bit so I took it off and asked my hot, buff, manly man husband to change it before he went to work. Of course, he forgot. So at six thirty at night, when I was ready to put Ada down after a long day at daycare, I noticed there was no sheet on the crib. "*$%!"? I yelled. "Darn it Rick!"
Then I remembered he was on a deadline at work and I tried to sympathize. Nope. Didn't work. So I sat Ada in the glider while I attempted to put the crib sheet on. You would think I was getting my butt kicked by a five-hundred-pound gorilla if you saw me in action. What a sight. I was struggling to lift the mattress, got the four corners secured and Ada was screaming at the tippy top of her lungs—like I just took her to the doctoress for her shots—and I was seconds away from tears when I channeled my anger into the fourth corner of the @#$%*^& sheet and it finally gave way. Whew! Breakdown narrowly averted.

Since the fourth corner was the worst, it made me hesitant to fix the corner of one of her sheets that I ripped while trying to put it on a few weeks ago. (We have four crib sheets since she is really good at soiling them). At least I can get that one on, sort of. I mean, it won't stay on but so what? Who needs crib sheets anyway?

Moral of the story: I CAN change a crib sheet—I don't LIKE to but I am ABLE. You can't always rely on your husband to do the things you hate to do just because you hate doing them. (He might hate doing them too.) And there is no use crying over tight crib sheets—unless it helps you get the fourth corner over the mattress. Then go for it.

A Day in the Life of Ada's Wardrobe

It's May 4, 2008.

6:30 A.M.
Ada wakes up wearing a plain white Onesie under her pajamas which Mom thinks resembles something Moses would wear back in the day, only pink with butterflies. Dad changes her into her first outfit for the day—a white Onesie with grey and pink stripped pants, white socks.

8 A.M.
She and Mom are hanging out on the couch, having breakfast and she throws up on Mom's teal shirt (Mom shirt #1) and herself. Ada outfit #2 for the day—Elephant Onesie with blue pants, same white socks.

9:30 A.M.
Ada throws up all over. It's time for a shower. Dad gets started, Mom passes Ada to Dad but before the hand off could happen, Baby poops on Mom's teal tank top (Mom shirt #2) and black shorts (Mom pants #1). While in the shower, she throws up on Dad. Mom towels her off, diapers her up and puts her in a Onesie for her nap.

11 A.M.
Jon, Dani and Eli arrive from Milwaukee and are ready for lunch. Ada finishes up her nap and Dad dresses her in Outfit #3 —a white Onesie and green Winnie the Pooh top and pants, with white Trumpette brand socks that look like Mary Janes. We pack her up and add her giraffe sun hat.

We enjoy a meal outside in the sun and decide to go to the Lincoln Park Zoo. But Ada needs something a bit heavier so we can carry her in the Baby Bjorn. Amazingly the green Pooh top and pants stayed clean while she was in them.

1 P.M.
We're ready for the zoo. Outfit #4—light pink fleece jogging suit over her Onesie and her giraffe sun hat. We make it the entire trip with just a bunch of drool on the burp cloth.

4:30 P.M.
We're home and ready to go to a new mom group once we change out of our hot fleece jogging suit and into something a bit cooler. On to Outfit #5—we keep the white Onesie and switch back to the grey and pink stripped pants (with a tiny spot of throw up on them but who cares.)

4:45 P.M.
She soils her diaper cover with a mass explosion but we are able to save the stripped pants, Onesie and socks.

5 P.M.
We arrive at the new mom group at Liz's house, and Mom notices something wet as she carries Ada in to meet the new moms. Ada poops and pees through her diaper cover and pants as we walk in. Her entire outfit is annihilated. Mom changes her into Outfit #6—cupcake Onesie and pink pants.

5:10 P.M.
Ada throws up all over. She hit Mom's brown Threadless t-shirt (Mom shirt #3). Mom strips down to her brown long-sleeve shirt and wipes Ada up.

5:25 P.M.
Ada spits up on her burp cloth and outfit.

5:40 P.M.
Repeat.

5:55 P.M.
Repeat.

6:15 P.M.
Repeat.

6:35 P.M.
Repeat.

6:45 P.M.
Repeat. Mom gives up with slobber on the shoulder of her
brown long-sleeve shirt (Mom shirt #4). Mom thanks other
moms and says it was nice to meet them all—yes, for the first
time! Nothing like a whole bunch of spit up on you to make a
good first impression.

7 P.M.
We arrive home and Ada throws up again, this time on Dad
(Dad shirt #1). We change her into pajamas (Outfit #7), and
she proceeds to throw up on them by the time Mom walks from
Ada's room to the kitchen to say "Hi" to Dad.

Total wardrobe ready for washing:
Pants—Pink Striped, Light Blue, Pink Solid
Onesies—White, Elephant, White, Cupcake
Burp cloths—Too many to count.
Mom's—Teal Shirt, Teal Tank Top, Black Shorts, Brown Shirt,
Brown Long-Sleeve Shirt
Dad's—Green Shirt
Diaper Covers—Pink, Royal Blue, Flowers, Light Blue
Socks—Surprisingly none. Normally they get covered in poop
during diaper changes. This was the miracle of the day.

Moral of the story: Spit happens, poop happens, pee happens
and all you can do about it is laundry, more laundry, laugh and
giggle.

Happy Mother's Day!

Before I became a mom, I used to think Mother's Day was just
another Hallmark holiday and another reason to make my
mom a card. My mom loves the homemade cards best—no
offense Hallmark. But now I have a whole new respect for
Mother's Day and for Father's Day too. It turns out, being a
parent is a lot of hard work and takes a lot of time, thought,
effort, and money. But it is so worth it in the end, even if I did
get thrown up on four times already this morning.

Being a mom isn't about being urped on all day. It's about
cuddle time, watching your baby learn and grow, and being
amazed about the milestones they reach. It's about spending
way too much time with family who can't get enough of the new

baby, and being overjoyed when they offer to babysit so you and your husband can go on your first date night in over four months—so what if date night means dinner, frozen custard, and hanging out at the local Target playing on the porch furniture and kissing on the loveseats. It's about falling even more in love with your spouse, and learning to manage the new shape your relationship takes. And it's about being loved by someone so tiny that you are responsible for bringing into this world. It's many more things too, but since I'm a mom, I'm short on time and have to run...

Moral of the story: Being a mom is one of the best things in the world. Be sure to appreciate your mom all year round because even if she makes it look easy, she sacrificed a lot for you. And do something nice for yourself if you are a mom—this is your chance so you better take it.

Time for Solids

Once a baby reaches a certain age, typically four to seven months, it's time to start them on solids. That doesn't mean you start filling their rotund Budda bellies with everything you can mash up and convince them to eat though. It means you start them with a teaspoon or so of rice cereal mixed with breast milk or formula. Then you gradually give them a bit more each day until they are having about two tablespoons daily. Then you can start introducing fruits and veggies the same way.

So my friend Natasha—I have to steal this story since it is so good—sent her hubby to the store to get some rice cereal for their baby, Linnea. She got a call from him at the store from the cereal aisle. "Honey, what kind of rice cereal do you want me to buy? They have rice flakes, rice puffs, or Rice Krispies?"
To which my friend Natasha replied, "Dear, are you in the baby food aisle?"
"No. Whole Foods doesn't have a baby food aisle."
"Yes, they do. Now go find someone who can help you find the baby food aisle and look for 'rice cereal' for babies." If left up to her husband, Linnea would be starting out with full blown Rice Krispies instead of the much more fine, single grain baby cereal that is simple to digest.

My point being that babies just don't come with an owner's

manual. But they should. There are many people that have gone before me and done this, so why can't one of them write it down and help a mother out! I'm off to buy a book on how to make my own baby food so that I can use it as a guide on how to introduce what foods when. A lot of it is common sense, if you already have a kid or know people who have kids. But sometimes this whole mom thing feels like being a pioneer in a new world—where the little people don't speak your language, spit up on you a lot, and make you change their stinky pants. Gesh!

Moral of the story: Be sure to make friends with moms who have kids older than yours so you can steal their tricks. Don't let your husband do the cereal shopping (or be very specific). And introduce solids slowly so as not to freak the kid out—i.e. save the steak for you and your spouse to enjoy.

Adjusting to a New Schedule

Last week was officially the first week of my new job. I quit my previous job when I got the feeling that they just weren't going to be very flexible with my new schedule and it wasn't where I wanted to be money and career wise anyway. So I decided to start my own marketing consulting firm and work out of my home. I was able to find a part-time daycare which was a miracle, and things were going great. I wasn't even really looking for a "real job" when a friend of mine called and asked about my situation. She had heard of a part-time position that might be right up my alley. I thought, well, I have one client for my consulting firm but it is going to take awhile to get this thing up and running and I'm not sure if I'm up for the challenge just yet. So, I decided to humor my friend, forwarded my resume along and waited to see what happened.

What happened was I started about two weeks later. Now I had a "real job" three days a week and a little more here and there when I could get to it. Ada could hang out in daycare those three days, I would get some "adult" time that was a much needed relief from her recent bouts of teething and gas and just overall "gosh it's hard being a baby" fussiness. And most importantly, I would get some balance in life—hopefully.

So these last two weeks I've had to get back into the swing of things and I realized that everything in life is exhausting, not just babies!

Thursday (the week before last) was my very first day. I tried to get going in the morning but boy was it ever hard. Figuring out what part of your work wardrobe still fits you is challenge #2 (getting out of bed is #1). Thankfully, my husband had flex time and could go to work anywhere between seven and nine and leave eight work hours later. He helped get Ada and me ready for our big day. Rick had worked late earlier in the week and earned a half day off for putting in so many late nights. What should have been a great opportunity for him to sleep in and relax didn't quite turn out that way.

Knowing that I needed to drop Ada off at eight, get to work at eight thirty, leave at four thirty and pick Ada up at five, I thought I'd drive to work my first day to make things easier. Little did I know that you really can't park anywhere near my new job unless you want to feed a meter all day or pay fourteen dollars for a spot. Yikes! I ended up parking at a meter a few blocks from the office and Rick had to come move the car back to the street Ada's daycare is on so that I could ride the El to pick her up. What a fiasco. But it all worked out. So much for Rick getting any sleep.

I had the weekend to recover—but I didn't recover much because Ada and I got sick with colds, she was teething and we spent Mother's Day at our parents' houses so we weren't in the comfort of our own homes to heal and reset our systems.

Monday came. We did some errands and prepared for our new schedule.

Tuesday came and we figured it out a bit better. Ada slept in which allowed me to get ready. But it really was a juggling act and when a baby was involved, you had to be flexible. If she wasn't ready to get up or wanted to eat when you were supposed to be in the car, it really messed up the timetables.

Wednesday was better. I even took snacks and my own lunch to work. I started to feel more comfortable disappearing into the bathroom for twenty-five minutes to pump after lunch. But boy was I ever tired once I got home. I was yawning all day and trying not to let the boss notice but it was pretty obvious since I work in an office with four people. You couldn't really hide easily. That night, in my exhaustion, I entertained friends for knitting club at my house. The social calendar must go on. Thursday was nice as I was already looking forward to the weekend and getting my four days with Ada and a weekend in my own bed. Wooohooo! What a relief it would be if I could just make it through the day. It started with Thursday treats and ended with lunch. Yes, lunch. Being the boss's birthday meant we had a long lunch which cut into my productivity but made the day fly by. Before I knew it, I was back on the El headed to get Ada. Then once she was in bed, more social time to catch up with a friend.

A big part of the adjustment of going back to work was only seeing my child for a few hours a day, if that. I got to see Ada from when I picked her up from daycare until she went to bed, and maybe an hour in the morning. Typically I fed her, cuddled a bit, maybe played and went for a short walk. Then it was time for her bedtime routine and I got prepared to do it all again the next day. I think the harder adjustment would be for parents who don't get home until the kids are ready for bed or already asleep. They would just get to see the kids on the weekends. That would be like having joint custody. Ugh.

Knowing how hard it was for me to adjust to this schedule makes me thankful for the arrangement I have. It's just another thing to think about when deciding to have kids—how much time would we get to see them and how could we make that work financially. It's sad that this is how the world works nowadays. All we can do is try our best to achieve some sort of balance in life, and try to get some rest.

Moral of the story: Not only is having a baby tough and a lot of work, but adjusting to life after having a baby is tough and a lot of work, and then you get to adjust to maybe going back to work, or "working" as a parent. Anyway you slice it, it's tough and tiring. I wish all parents the best of luck.

Teething, Still

This is the face of teething.

Ada miserable, in pain, chewing on Dad's hand for some relief. Dad, equally miserable, in pain from listening to her struggle with her teeth, knowing that the teething medicine isn't working, the Tylenol isn't working, the cuddling, bouncing, shushing, kissing, massaging, and ice chewy things aren't working either.

For as easy as pregnancy was, and as quick as my labor was, and the fact that she wasn't colicky, and I don't have stretch marks, I'm getting my just desserts now that she is teething.

If only we can make it a few more days, weeks, months. How long do these damn things take already?

Moral of the story: Teething still sucks, it has thus far, it always will, and I'd still rather deal with her screaming than give her "a bit of rum on her gums" to take care of it.

I Wish I Had Known

There is no "right" way to parent. Every child/mother/family is different and you do what works and what feels right, especially when it comes to sleep. Even if your mom/mother-in-law/friends/old lady at the mall would do it differently, don't stress over the things other people find important. Do what is right for you.

Despite how hard and challenging motherhood is (and there are brutally difficult times), it is all worth it. Look at every moment as the present because soon all the hard times are nothing but a memory.

To be prepared for what happens "if"... If your baby has complications that keep them in the Neonatal Intensive Care Unit (NICU), you may not be able to take them home with you when you are released. Know that it is okay if they need to spend more time in the hospital even though you are back home. It is the best place for them and there will be plenty of time to introduce them to all of your family and friends once they are ready.

To be open to the challenges of recovery once the baby is here. No one wants to scare a pregnant woman, so often times you don't hear how rough it is. From emotions being out of whack (even more so than during pregnancy), to the swelling "down there", to simple trips to the bathroom taking twenty minutes. Give yourself time to heal, be prepared to ask for help and know that it probably will get ugly—but it is temporary and so worth it.

That for some moms, falling in love with their baby isn't immediate. It might take some time and that's okay. Just do your best and the love part will come on its own. Give it time.

How hard and lonely motherhood can be. Some women cry for weeks and have trouble adjusting to motherhood. It is good to find a mom group, or friends who already have kids, who you can call and get advice from once you have your child. You'll need them far more than you can ever imagine.

How temporary each stage is. Sleep deprivation, hormones, pain, and teething. None of it lasts forever and it does get better.

If you don't have family around, find some close friends and ask them if they'll be willing to help you out. And if they offer, take them up on babysitting, meals, and anything else they volunteer. You'll need it.

How much intentional effort needs to be put into teaching a baby to sleep. We think most babies just sleep naturally, and that those who don't simply outgrow that stage and start sleeping on their own. It can be a shock to realize that babies have to learn how to sleep properly. It is best to research a sleep strategy while you're still pregnant and getting some sleep. Then you will already have an idea of what to do before you become so sleep deprived that you can't even see straight.

What a doula and a midwife are and how they can help you during your pregnancy. Know that your doctor, the one you've been seeing for the last eight months or so, may or may not be the one to deliver your baby. It might be helpful to have a doula or midwife with you in case your doctor can't be. That way you'll have some consistency.

How much having a baby changes your relationship with your spouse, family and friends. You now play the role of mother in addition to wife, lover and whatever else might be on the list. Be sure to keep the lines of communication open and check in with your spouse often to see how things are going and what adjustments need to be made. Family might demand more of you now that you have a baby; they might want to see you more often and need more of your time. And some of your friendships will grow stronger while others will fade and new ones will form. Just be open to the changes and do your best to go with the flow.

How much having a baby changes your sex life. By way of the baby interrupting you, being too tired, not finding time because you haven't found your new life balance, or just healing differently from your pre-baby body.

How challenging and expensive it is to find child care. Nanny? Daycare? Stay-at-home mom/dad? Part-time? Full-time? Will my employer be flexible? Start early and plan to give yourself as many options as possible. You won't know until you've been caring for the baby for a few weeks whether you'll be able to leave them at daycare/with a nanny or not. Try to give yourself enough financial cushion to keep your options open and get creative.

Moral of the story: There is a lot to think about before you have kids. Try your best to be prepared and know that you'll get by with the help of your friends, new and old.

Just This Once, Can I?

Yet another challenge of parenthood is the whole debate of "When is it okay to leave the baby alone?" As in, I have to run into the house because I forgot something, can I leave the baby in the car in the garage/driveway? What if I live in the city and the car is right out front? Or, I just have to run into the post office to pick something up and she's sleeping in the back seat. Do I have to disturb her? Or, she's napping and I need to run (literally) next door to get an egg. Do I have to take her with me?

These situations come up on a daily basis and it's a judgement call. But there is a fine line between what is okay and what the law considers child endangerment.

There are the people who leave the baby in the car seat to run in to pick up a prescription. The neighborhood ladies who get together to play cards and bring their baby monitors and then check up on the kids every hour to make sure they are okay. Those who live in a high rise and go downstairs to do the laundry while the baby naps quietly above. And those who never ever leave the baby unattended.

I think it all has to do with what you are comfortable with and how safe you feel your baby can be without you. You hear of cars being stolen with kids in the back seat, homes catching fire while the parents stepped next door, and children being kidnapped. Is it worth the risk?

Recently, a woman near Chicago was accused of child endangerment when she stepped fifteen feet away from her car to take her two older kids into a Walmart to drop off coins they had collected and were donating to a charity during the holidays. Her baby was asleep in the back seat and the car was within her line of vision. Someone who noticed the car, and the baby in the back, immediately called police and the woman was charged with child endangerment. Everyone in her town considered her guilty from the very start. It wasn't until the case was heard that the charges were dismissed. Is it worth the ridicule and potential felony charges?

And a friend of mine didn't think much of doing laundry in the basement of her building until someone asked her what she would do if she got stuck in the elevator while her daughter was upstairs alone? I can tell you straight away that I would panic. I'd call everyone and their mother until I found someone to go check on her until I got rescued. But I can't blame my friend for not being in "what if" mode all of the time. I'm guilty of doing laundry in the basement one floor below my unit while the baby is sleeping. What's the difference between that and having a two-story house in the suburbs? If I get locked in the basement, how is that different from being locked out of your house if you go to grab the mail from the box near the street?

I once called my husband to ask if I needed to drag the car seat and Ada into the alderman's office eight feet from the car door when both his office and the car would be in plain sight of me at all times. The errand was to last one minute and his front desk is two feet from the door with glass windows clearly displaying my car. He said, "Yep, you gotta take her in with you. Better safe than sorry. I know it's a pain in the butt but if you don't and something happens to her, you'll regret it for the rest of your life." And he's right. But instead of taking her in with me, I flagged down some nice woman who was heading into the alderman's office and asked her to drop my stuff off for me. Then I sat there and watched her hand it to the woman behind the counter. They all looked at me like I was a freak even though I tried to explain that I had a baby in the back seat. And then as I started to pull out of the parking spot, another mother was trying to hold open the door while dragging her big jogging stroller into the lobby to do the same thing.

Another instance was while having dinner and playing a game

with friends we all decided we'd go across the street to get some ice cream. We debated who was going and someone suggested we all go. I said, "Sure that sounds great." Then my husband looked at me as I put my arm into my coat sleeve and said, "Honey, one of us has to stay here with the baby." I had completely forgotten that she even existed since she'd been asleep for an hour and hadn't made a peep. So I stayed behind and twiddled my thumbs until they brought back a shake for me.

I guess my rule of thumb is:
1) Absolutely (almost) never leave her in the car unattended—maybe if I lived in a really small town and she was in the driveway and I was going to go double check that I locked the front door or get my sunglasses from just inside the door.
2) Never leave her more than one flight away from you—I think in a fire, that's as far as I could even consider getting in order to save her and myself. My mom had a rule that all of her kids had to live in the same part of the house as her, i.e. the bedrooms all had to be next to one another so she could get to them should the house catch fire and that always stayed with me.
3) Avoid having doors that lock between you and your baby whenever possible, and make sure you have keys. This would include elevators, which I don't really like to begin with.
4) Don't ever leave your property without someone watching your child. The basement is one thing, the mailbox is another, dropping something off to a neighbor within a shout of your house is pushing it unless you are a really fast runner.
5) And even though the whole taking the baby monitor next door while you hang out with friends is tempting, just hire a babysitter to watch a movie or sleep on your couch while the baby sleeps. It's worth the peace of mind.

Moral of the story: Safety first. Don't be lazy when caring for your child. And avoid jail time since it's even harder to be a parent behind bars.

Pregnancy Rules

I have a rule I try to stick to whenever possible when pregnant in the city:

Never ride the El train unless you've gone to the bathroom

within ten minutes of boarding the train, have a bottle of water and a snack with you, have a cell phone, and are desperate. Why? Because the El trains are always breaking down and you don't want to be the "Pregnant woman removed from train and rushed to hospital after being stranded for four hours on the Brown line" in the newspaper. There always seems to be one of those women. And it is typically ninety degrees on the train, and everyone is packed in like sardines and no one is "Sure" if you know what I mean. I'd much rather take a cab or ride the bus for Pete's sake. Hitchhiking would be safer. Lucky for me, one of the few times I did take the train while pregnant was the Fourth of July and I was on the only train line leaving the loop that didn't lose power for a few hours. And yes, there was a pregnant woman on one of those other train lines that ended up in the paper the next day.

To reinforce this, my boss told me his wife was one of those women when she was pregnant. She got stuck on one of the trains while it was underground. After four hours of trying to reach her—cell phones don't work when you're down under— she finally popped up out of a man hole. With my luck my belly would be so big that I wouldn't fit through the man hole.

Let's just not go there.

Moral of the story: Be safe when you're "with child". Be sure you have reliable transportation. And travel with the necessities so that you don't overheat, dehydrate, starve, or otherwise injure yourself or your unborn child.

Ten Things Potential Parents Should Know

Babies need a lot of stuff—no really. A lot. Like a crazy lot, a lot.

Babies are expensive—no really. Really expensive. They go through clothes every five minutes. And diapers, my oh my how they go through diapers! And wipes!

Daycare is really expensive—ridiculously so. And nannies aren't any cheaper.

Sex is never the same—unless you currently worry about

constantly being interrupted by a screaming baby. Even then, no.

Laundry never stops. As soon as you get everything clean, the baby will pee, poop or spit up on whatever they are wearing.

Hospitals charge an insane amount of money to deliver your baby, even if you have the baby "au natural".

Giving birth involves a lot of gross bodily fluids. A lot. Like a crazy lot, a lot. It is not for the squeamish.

New moms have their very own type of Tendonitis that appears in your wrist called "De Quervain's Tendonitis" from lifting the baby repeatedly. It goes away eventually.

Babies cry. A lot. They completely depend on you all of the time.

Being a parent is the coolest thing ever and worth all the crap you have to go through to make it work.

Moral of the story: As a parent, you'll constantly learn as you go. No amount of preparation can ever ready you for this experience.

Pumping at Work

We all know it was just a matter of time before something entertaining came from me pumping at work. And finally it has.

I started the week off by remembering my pump, which is always my main fear since my chest would surely explode. I even remembered the tubing, power cord, hands-free tube top, shields and milk containers. It wasn't until I was done pumping that I realized I had forgotten the lids to the milk containers. Normally I would just pop off the connectors and shields, seal up the bottles and be done with it. But not today. Oh, no.

Thankfully, I do keep (or try to keep) a few milk storage bags with me for fear that I'll forget the containers. But... as I was transferring the measly contents of my pumping efforts—a whopping five ounces—from the containers to the plastic bag, I somehow managed to spill half an ounce on the counter top. At least I was further along in the process to where this stuff wasn't as much of a scarce resource as it once was. I no longer freaked out over a little spilled milk since I had some backup stocked in the freezer. Speaking of... the other item I forgot was the cold pack to keep the milk cold until I got home. Luckily I pumped after noon and got home just after five so it stayed good, in theory, during that time. But in my infinite wisdom, I decided to put two ice cubes straight from the freezer into the cold compartment of the breast pump bag to keep the milk cool. Little did I know that that compartment wasn't really waterproof at all. As I was sitting on the El for my ride home—yes sitting during rush hour which was a treat—I noticed two wet spots on the thighs of my pants. I sprung a leak! No, it was just my breast pump bag that was slowly dribbling on me. I quickly moved it to the floor and continued reading my book. Crisis averted. At least I was wearing jeans instead of some trendy white pants. It could have been so much worse.

Moral of the story: Medela still hasn't figured out how to design their pumps with moms in mind. It is wise to make checklists for the contents of your breast pump bag, diaper bag, and purse—and double check it before you leave home. And know that motherhood is a state of constant change—all you can do is get used to it.

Memorial Day Spit-Up-A-Thon

I'm not sure about the rest of the world, but today was a great day to live in Chicago. We had the most beautiful weather for this incredible holiday weekend. First of all, I'm thankful to all those who gave their lives for our freedom. I'm also thankful that we made it through today and got Ada to bed by eight. During holiday weekends, kids tend to get thrown off their daily routines. Ada actually had a good routine until about four in the afternoon when she went into a coughing and throwing up spell that lasted on and off until we got home after seven. She had two naps in the morning, one on the lawn while we cooked out with friends, and then something happened that made her life miserable. Okay, not her life really as much as it made things awkward as she threw up all over the front of my shirt, her first outfit, second outfit, four burp cloths, two bibs, etc. I spent the rest of the afternoon in a tank top playing board games with friends. She spent it in nothing but a diaper and a bib alternating between eating, throwing up and coughing. And not just an "ah hem" cough. I mean a "Heeech, Hack" guttural cough that sounded like she could launch a loogie ten feet. Disgusting.

Despite all of the coughing and the upset tummy, I will say that she thoroughly enjoyed being outside for a nice cookout, as you can see.

Moral of the story: When you have a baby, invest in a really big umbrella, baby sunblock, a sun hat, tons of burp cloths, and an outdoor blanket. Remember to always travel with all of those things so that you are prepared for warm weather fun. And try to pack an extra shirt for yourself or at the very least, always dress in layers or only visit friends who are your size or larger so you can borrow something from them or their husbands when your shirt or pants are destroyed by your child.

Ada's Adventures in Eating

All I can do is hope and wish and dream that Ada rediscovers her happy time soon. I know it's getting old. Her daycare knows it's getting really old—especially when you have a handful of other kids screaming at you on a daily basis. But I'm honestly not sure what else I can do to make her happier right now. I wish there was a magic potion I could give her but, I don't believe in using hard liquor on a child this small—even if she is big for her age.

What I have tried so far is to start her on solids and wait it out. As each day passes, we're slowly inching closer to her first (and second and third) tooth popping up. I can feel them more and more each day. All Rick and I can say at this point is "This is why babies are so cute." And she is cute. And worth it. But come on already! Enough with the fussiness. I'm told it gets better soon. Wish us all luck and patience.

Moral of the story: You're not alone if your kid is a hot mess like mine.

June

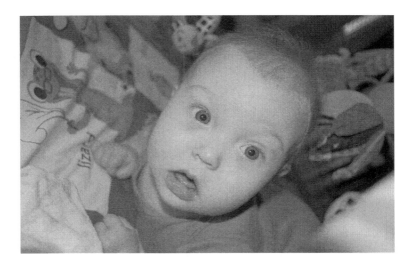

Happy Birthday Mom

My first birthday as a mom is here. What a day filled with emotion. Some good, some bad. Overall, a day for reflection. Being a Monday, I didn't go in to work. Being the day after we threw a birthday BBQ at our house, I had a lot of work to do.

Pre-mommyhood, birthday parties were about going out to the clubs and getting crazy with friends—or in our case, having our thirty closest friends come over for a crazy night in. It has typically been a day for me to get wild and free and be silly. This year however, I feel things have changed a bit. They didn't necessarily have to, but they did. Instead of a house party into the wee hours, I opted for a daytime BBQ and was in bed at nine. Instead of a small array of chocolate martinis, I had a few glasses of water... and several desserts. And instead of me being the subject of the photos, Ada took center stage. I don't think there are any photos of me at my birthday party. Granted, I also decided to do a shared birthday party with Ada since she'll be six months in about a week. I believe that birthdays should not be overshadowed by holidays and I can set whatever traditions I want since the majority of Americans can't tell you why we celebrate most of the holidays we do... hence this doubling as

Ada's half-birthday party. So things changed a bit, but in a good way.

The party was a blast. It was great to see so many friends come out to celebrate. I ate some fabulous desserts and got to spend a little time with a lot of good friends. I think it was similar to a wedding or baby shower where there are so many people and you are the host, or just the one person everyone has in common, so everyone needs you to make decisions—Do we need more meat? Do you want someone to get more ice? Should we put out more cupcakes? But it is a challenge to host your birthday party when you are busy playing mommy at the same time. I am blessed to have a child that doesn't mind strangers and can be held by many, and passed around pretty well, but I'm also still nursing so there were a few times during the party that I had to disappear into the nursery to try to get Ada to eat. It's tough greeting your guests as they come in and leave when you're exposing your left boob. Maybe that would have made the party even more wild and crazy though—I hadn't thought of that.

That was yesterday. Not my actual birthday but the day before my birthday. Today, my actual birthday, I got to wake up to a messy house and a sizable list of mommy duties and chores. But I must say, it beats a day with a hangover hands down.

In my reflections of turning a year older, I look back on twenty-eight and have hopes for twenty-nine. I'm thankful for my girlfriends who took me to lunch and dinner today to celebrate in Rick's absence—he had to work late on my birthday. I'm thankful for my beautiful daughter with whom I spent the entire day and I must say, she took a nice morning nap, didn't fuss much, behaved well at lunch at a restaurant and while on errands, slept in the car and at Aunt Anne's house, ate well, and made a great doorstop as I managed the inner and outer vestibule doors today with the stroller and diaper bag—venturing out twice. She pooped solid poops today since she started solids—happy birthday mom—and not once, not twice, but three times. And she didn't even give me grief about going to bed at eight fifteen instead of her usual six thirty to seven thirty window.

And, since it was my birthday, she even let me read my favorite stories to her before bed. How lucky am I?

Moral of the story: A lot of things change when you have a baby, but they aren't all bad. Sure you see friends globetrotting and spending lavishly on frivolous things, but I have a baby. And I wouldn't change that for the world. Her smile just before she went to bed tonight was worth every tough moment I've had these last six months, and I'd do it again in a heartbeat.

Daycare Drama

I'm not one to over think things much, or I don't think I am anyway. So I've been pretty confused as to why everyone keeps asking me "How's daycare going?" "How's Ada doing at daycare?" "Is Ada adjusting to daycare alright?" I mean, daycare is daycare. She goes to daycare, I go to work. I pick her up, she urps on me, we go home. She eats, goes to bed and we repeat. Then our four-day "weekend" comes, we try to stick to a schedule, and we do it all over again come Tuesday.

I've only known half-a-dozen parents who have taken their kids to daycare and I've never really known other parents who didn't have it go okay so I don't have any preconceived ideas about how it should or shouldn't be. And Ada has been really fussy at daycare but I just assumed that was her teething or one of her colds or her sinus infection, or just a rough day. So last week I was a bit shocked when her daycare said we need to find a strategy to improve her experience at daycare. I'm not sure what that means and I feel funny admitting it but, we have a parent-daycare conference scheduled for this week to discuss how things are going. At six-months old I already feel like she's dragging me into the principal's office. My goodness!

So far, I think I've been rather relaxed about daycare and not too worried about what she's doing all day since I know she's in good hands and I trust her care takers. But since she has been having a bunch of fussy days and there isn't much consistency between how she behaves at home vs. daycare, it turns out that this whole daycare thing is really stressful. Because she isn't getting reports of having a lot of "Happy Ada" time, now I'm concerned that it might not be going okay. She might not be adjusting to it as well as I thought. Which, as a mom, makes me feel like I am failing her and I constantly wonder if she is crying all day while I am at work. I know when I'm home with her, she always has a reason for crying—mainly her teeth are hurting—

but I can run through the wet, dirty, overtired, hot, hungry, gassy, bored, teething, uncomfortable list and figure it out. Occasionally she just needs a cuddle but for the most part, I'd say 99% of the time she has a reason to be ticked off at this age—unlike before when you really just never knew. So I'm extra concerned that she may be crying just because she doesn't like going to daycare. Maybe she's secretly allergic to other kids... hmmmm... that would be bad if we have more kids huh...

Among all of the things I must learn as a parent, I now get to include how to make sure she is adjusting well to daycare—or the more scary alternative of finding an alternative to daycare while living in the city. To add to my list of things no one ever tells you before you have kids... not only is daycare expensive, but there aren't many options—all having pluses and minuses—and they tend to have wait lists to get your kid accepted if you live in the city. If things don't start to improve with daycare, I'll have to look into a nanny share, other daycares, another mom who is looking to take in another kid during the day, a college student who needs a summer job a few days a week, or becoming a stay-at-home mom full time—which would be a serious last resort for me and financially not really viable.

On top of the stress of thinking she might not be her happy self all day long, here I am with the feeling that my kid is the one that daycare just can't wait to get rid of at five. "It's Ada's mom, Thank God! Finally we can get rid of this screaming child!" I don't want to be that parent. I don't want her to be that kid who screams all day and is miserable. Not only do I not want the daycare staff to look at me like I've brought a monster into the world, but I don't want her to be unhappy. She's my little monster, and I love her. I'll admit there are days where I think it would be nice to send her back or give her away, but I don't really mean it. It's just a nice fantasy to have when she has been screaming at me for an hour because her teeth hurt and she's tired because she couldn't take a nap because she was coughing and couldn't sleep because her teeth hurt and the Orajel wore off already and she's tired...and I'm tired of her screaming at me.

Who knew?

This story is to be continued... we'll see how it ends up. Either way, Ada needs to be somewhere she is comfortable, happy, and enjoys going to three days a week. Hopefully we'll be closer to figuring that out by the end of the week for her sake and for ours.

Moral of the story: Parent-teacher conferences aren't just for school-aged children. Even an infant can be unruly.

Accentuate the Positives

Many of my stories have an "it's tough being a mom" theme so today I decided to sing a different note. Don't worry, I won't really sing.

The positives of having a baby:

Her smiling face makes it all worthwhile.

You get to take credit for all of the awesome things she does—like when Ada started sucking her thumb, albeit momentarily. Dad's pretty excited about that.

She's super fun to cuddle with. And when she holds on to you for fear of falling, it almost feels like a hug. It's pretty awesome to think that this little thing thinks you are the most important person in the world.

You are proud of every little milestone, and feel the need to share it with friends—"She's pooping solids! Yippee! We're so proud."

When she whacks at the spoon as you try to feed her and sends food flying through the air you can make easy, quick jokes—"Her father taught her that." "She's in training for the 2020 Olympics. By then, Food Fighting should be a competitive sport."

You get random smiles and extra attention walking down the street with a baby.

When she is busy entertaining herself on her play mat or in her bouncy seat, you get some free time.

If nursing, you are bustier and able to eat a lot since you are eating for two.

Holding her and lifting her up and down gives you buff arm muscles so you look great in sleeveless tops.

Redecorating your house as part of baby proofing and making room for a nursery can be fun. (Note: I didn't say "remodeling" but "redecorating" instead.)

Using the fact that you have kids as an excuse for having a messy house.

The feeling of accomplishment when someone compliments your parenting skills—"She sleeps through the night! That's awesome! You guys must be doing something right."

The feeling of good fortune when you realise how rare it is for your child to sleep through the night.

Forming closer relationships with relatives since they all want to spend time with the baby.

As a form of entertainment, babies are excellent performers. Watching her expression as she eats a food she doesn't like is quite fun. And the enormous smile you get just from shaking her legs or blubbering your lips can entertain for hours.

She's a great reason to get the camera you've always wanted.

And how awesome is it that I created a new person to roam on the earth? I think that is the best part.

Moral of the story: Kids are a ton of work but they bring so many good times, memories, and laughs that it is all worthwhile a million times over. So get to procreating already!

Iowa

I'm originally from Iowa, and I went to the University of Iowa for my undergraduate degree. My dad has been a football season ticket holder for as long as I can remember. And as a little girl, I slept with a Herky the Hawk stuffed animal every night. He played the Iowa fight song from a music box sewn in his torso.

As a mother now, it is hard to watch the news about the floods in Iowa without thinking "What if that were my family?" I saw a photo of a woman carrying a baby about Ada's size while she was on the second story deck of an apartment in Coralville that already had water halfway up the first floor. I can't imagine having to move into a shelter with your kids and then worry about getting diapers, wipes, baby food, formula, and clothing for them too.

Farms are destroyed, pets lost, families displaced, but it couldn't have happened to a nicer state of people. Iowa will rebuild, but unlike other disaster areas in the US, they'll have fun doing it. Being a marketing person, I worried that this would hurt Iowa's current campaign trying to draw people to the state. Now I feel this whole situation will only reinforce that message by showing compelling stories of neighbors helping neighbors rebuild and get through the "Floods of '08". It will take time, but Iowa will be just fine.

Go Hawks!

Moral of the story: Natural disasters will come and go. Be sure to form a network of friends and family in case you ever need help. And don't hesitate to help someone in need as you never know when you'll need that good deed to come back around.

Daycare Update Two

As I left it, we were headed to a meeting with daycare to see if things were going to improve and what we could be doing differently to make everyone's life better. We went into the meeting with a list of things we were concerned about, and a list of things that daycare had mentioned as issues we needed to deal with. To be fair and politically correct about it, I think both sides of the situation—Rick and I as the parents, and Ada's daycare—put a lot of effort into making things work. The problem is, Ada is a one-on-one baby when it comes to being babysat by someone other than her parents. She doesn't like to be left alone to play on her mat or bouncy seat for too long—

even though she'll do that for us at home—she doesn't like to sleep in a Pack 'n Play at daycare—even though she only naps in her crib at home. She just didn't adjust well to the situation. Now we know and can move on.

My advice to anyone dealing with a similar situation—and the lesson I've learned from all of this is... You are the parent. Your decision and opinion is the only one that matters in the end. Get a spine and stand up for what you believe in. Listen to your gut, fight for whatever your gut tells you to do, and don't let other people boss you around when it comes to caring for your child. This is a hard thing to do, as I've struggled with it and finally snapped after about three weeks of knowing that things just weren't right for Ada.

As for the gory details, we had the meeting, listened to the daycare's suggestions for possible ways to make things better for Ada and her experience and it backfired. (This brings me to my next story on how to deal with a nursing mother and what not to ever suggest to them.) What we tried was only feeding Ada from a bottle, having a strict morning routine, and reducing the amount of time when we had physical contact with Ada (nursing, carrying, cuddling, etc.). We also learned that daycare wasn't feeding her to sleep, while I was—even though I was trying to break her of that habit since it is bad for her oral hygiene. The good thing that came from all of this was that she doesn't need to be feed to sleep anymore and the morning routine helped get her into more of a daily routine and she seems to be happier with that. The bad news is that this new routine didn't really improve her behavior at daycare. Now I must add that we had this meeting on a Monday. They implemented their changes and spent more time with her that week. Then that weekend I implemented the changes on our end. Come the following Tuesday, I was a wreck. In the process of not nursing Ada in order to reduce the bond she had with me (I now know this is just asinine so don't even start with me—touchy subject) my milk production dropped. Low. As in, I went from supplying daycare with twenty ounces or more each day to having three ounces to send to daycare with her that Wednesday. Knowing things were bad, I contacted my lactation consultant and we had a heart to heart.

Long story shortened up a bit, I realized that things at daycare weren't getting any better and I didn't want Ada in a daycare that didn't believe in holding her, giving her the one-on-one attention that she needed, and suggested that I try to break my bond with her so that it was easier for her to be "dealt with" at daycare. It turned out that six months was a pretty critical time in a baby's life and one in which she really needed to have a strong bond with her parents in order to develop a sense of trust and to combat separation anxiety.

So the drama unfolded Tuesday night when I asked daycare to feed Ada a mix of breast milk and soy formula on Wednesday since I didn't have enough milk. Ada had had a rotten day that day and the report wasn't good. Then daycare said they didn't want to be the first one to give Ada formula with her breast milk on Wednesday. I didn't feel that was very accommodating so that was the straw that broke the camel's back. I got into the car to come home, called Rick and told him we were done. Then we called to tell daycare we quit and friends and family have watched Ada for last two weeks. She has been so much happier for it.

Moral of the story: Get a spine. Be your child's advocate because no one else will. And follow your gut feelings for everything in life.

Dealing with a Nursing Mother

Nursing mothers are a delicate species. There are rumors that the women from La Leche are a bit hard core, some might say crazy, but I'd describe them more as passionate about nursing. Breast milk, as I've covered before, is insanely good for your child. It has tons of benefits, nursing is a major bonding experience, and it's way cheaper than formula. Nursing, as an experience, changes a mother. I must admit, I was temporarily insane for a few hours last week when I thought I might have to stop nursing abruptly. It happens to the best of us. Now let me give the rest of the world a little bit of insight into the mind of a nursing mother and how best not to set them off.

When I became pregnant, I was hopeful that nursing would take, I'd be able to produce enough milk, Ada would latch on, it wouldn't be too painful, yadda yadda. There are a ton of issues that go into the decision to nurse. It is a very personal choice, and one that is highly influenced by spouses, a woman's workplace, friends, and peers. In the US, it isn't as popular or widely accepted as it is in foreign countries since somewhere someone decided that potentially seeing a little boob exposed in public was a bad thing—definitely wasn't a man making that decision.

Lucky for me, Ada took to nursing and it turns out I have good boobs. Which was shocking since everyone made fun of me for being small busted as a teenager and I've been a bit self conscious ever since. Now I'm a temporary C cup and don't know what to do with them. But I digress...

Rule 1: If you know someone who is nursing, be supportive of her decision. If you are uncomfortable with her whipping out the boob in your presence, you can mention it to her in private or leave the room when she is feeding. Chances of you seeing actual boob are not likely, and if you do, consider it a free scene from an R rated movie and get over it. It's part of the miracle of life. You'll understand one day when you have kids and if you don't, then you're weird.

Rule 2: Do not to ever suggest that she switch to formula unless it is something she really wants to do and your position is one of saying, "Don't worry that you have to supplement with formula/stop nursing. Babies are brought up on formula all of the time and it doesn't make you a bad mom. The fact that you tried nursing is more than a lot of people and something you can be proud of." This follows rule number one by being supportive.

Rule 3: Never suggest to a nursing mother that she stop nursing and bottle feed the breast milk to the baby in order to break the mother/child bond so it is easier for others to take care of the baby. That's just stupid. Babies need their mothers. It is their time together and I don't believe you can spoil your child by nursing them.

Rule 4: Never suggest a mother supplement formula for breast milk in order to make the baby less gassy once they are a few months old. The baby should adjust to the mother's milk after about a month so if they are gassy, it isn't likely due to what the mom is eating.

Rule 5: If you aren't an expert on nursing, or haven't at the very least experienced it yourself, don't ever tell a nursing mother what to do. Just don't.

Rule 6: Don't ever tell a mother they need to go to the bathroom to breastfeed unless you are going to provide them with a comfortable chair and sanitary conditions for them to nurse privately. No one should be banished to a dirty public restroom in order to not disturb the other patrons. That's crap.

Rule 7: Be sensitive to a woman who is weaning her child off the boob. It is a very emotional time. I've got it in my head that I will nurse Ada for about a year. That seems to be a common goal for moms. Some make it a few weeks, some go for six months, I'm shooting for a year since that is when she can switch to whole cow's milk. Mooo. One of my main motivations is that I don't want to pay for formula since it is so expensive. The other reason, which I realized only after my milk supply was threatened, is that I really like our time spent nursing because I have an excuse to cuddle with Ada. And if someone else is holding her, I have an excuse to take her back anytime I want because, "She needs to nurse." It's great.

Rule 8: Encourage your workplace and stores you shop at to be mom friendly and provide amenities for nursing moms. It's difficult enough to nurse but even worse when you have to try to find somewhere you feel you can whip out your boob in order to get your kid to stop screaming in public. Just adjusting to motherhood is tough but once you add nursing, you're on a whole new level in the game of life.

I will say that mother's shouldn't nurse their children to sleep, or should at least try not to since it can be bad for their teeth in the long run and they can get ear infections too. But it is easier said than done and takes time to change that habit.

And a mini lesson in milk production. Even though your doctor/lactation consultant/friend's-mother's-grandfather's-dog-that-has-since-passed-away-and-been-reincarnated-as-a-fairy-godmother says that you can go on a birth control with estrogen, even if it is localized like the Nuva Ring, there is still a good chance it will decrease your milk production, especially if you are thin. Stress can also dramatically lower your milk production. And when your child starts solids, your milk supply will drop. So when you start nursing, it is best if you can pump a little each day to store in the freezer for when/if your milk supply dwindles. If it does, don't worry. It can, and likely will, come back. In my case, I thought I was done for since I only had three ounces left. But then I stayed home with Ada for a day and nursed, pumped like crazy, de-stressed a bit, got off the estrogen birth control and things have been much better. It really helps to reduce stress if you just go out and buy a formula you'd be willing to give your child mixed with some breast milk in case you ever run out. Then you know that even if things go poorly with your supply, your child won't starve to death for lack of milk, even if it is formula—which isn't a four letter word mind you. It's just really expensive.

As an afterthought to all of this, be sure you have friends who have nursed that you can ask all kinds of questions. I asked several friends what to do the other day and I got three completely different answers. It was a great way for me to realize that it is my choice whether or not I nurse, for how long, how often, etc. One friend said, "Stop nursing if it is too much work, too stressful, not enjoyable, etc."

Another said, "Don't worry, you can get your milk production back up. You don't have to give up yet if you don't want to, but it is okay if you do."

And yet another said, "You can always do a combo of nursing and supplement your milk with formula until you decide to stop nursing or continue full force. Some women only nurse once or twice a day for months and give their babies formula or cow's milk for the rest of their feedings." All of which was great advice and made me feel that I didn't have to make a drastic decision to stop nursing right away.

Moral of the story: Don't mess with a nursing momma, be supportive of the ones you know, and never give them advice unless you know what you're talking about.

Swish and Spin

Until now, Ada's diapers haven't been all that nasty. But recently, she started solids, which means she also started pooping solids. And since we use cloth diapers that changes things a bit. We're trying to adjust and I'm sure it will be a bit of a process. It seems to be going well so far.

The good news: Breastfed babies don't poop a lot. Some poop everyday, some poop once a week. It isn't like they poop in every diaper all day long, so you won't be relegated to the bathroom to clean poopy diapers every five minutes.

The bad news: Poopy diapers stink. And you have to rinse them out before you wash them in the laundry machine—unless you use a diaper service, but even then you should at least remove the majority of your baby's handy work.

The solution: We've decided to change the poopy diaper, take it to the toilet, swish it around, flush the solid material while we hold the diaper in the water, then rinse the diaper in the sink and put it into the diaper pail. Since the diaper pail smells more funky than ever before, we're attempting to use a "wet pail" instead of a "dry pail" meaning that we fill the pail with water and let the diapers soak in it until it is time to wash them—which is about every other day. This is supposed to cut the acid of the urine and contain the funky smell a bit. If you have a top loading washer, you can dump the water in with the diapers when you do the wash. I have a front loading machine so I can either drain it in the tub and pull out some rubber gloves to transfer it to the machine, or I can run downstairs and wash them in the coin machine. Not pleasant but I'm doing what I can to save money and the environment.

I'm also going to try out the cloth wipes for when she has a poopy diaper. I think they will be easy to use and I can throw them into the "wet pail" with the diapers instead of throwing them into the garbage can and having to take the garbage out every time she poops.

Another tip—we tend to use disposable diapers when we travel since we already have to take a gazillion things with us when we travel with the baby. Otherwise you have to take the diapers, covers, wipes, and a bag to transport all of the dirty diapers back home with you, and you may have to do laundry while you are out and about. We've done it both ways but find that for convenience it is a bit less bulk to use disposables. That and I fear having to swish and spin in a public toilet.

Moral of the story: Cloth diapers are a bit more work and a bit more disgusting, unless you have a diaper service, but it really isn't that bad. You have to deal with the poop either way so just take a deep breath and try not to breathe—or be mature like me and yell "not it" as soon as you smell the baby bomb, then pass her off to your husband.

Lockdown

Many people refer to a wife as a "ball-and-chain" when a guy gets married. Sometimes I feel that way about having a baby. I guess I didn't really realize that once you have a baby, you can't run out after they go to sleep unless you have a babysitter or someone is home to watch them. Ada goes to sleep around seven now so I am kind of under a sort of lockdown from seven on. It doesn't matter that she won't be up until seven in the morning and doesn't need anything for the rest of the night. Someone still has to be here while she sleeps, just in case.

The other day I compared having a baby to that contest radio stations have every once and a while to win a car. You know, the one where you have to have some part of your body touching the car at all times and the last person left touching the car in the end wins? Babies are kind of like that. Once they go to sleep, someone always has to be home. But you don't win a car in the end and you can get up to go pee or get a snack so in many ways it is better than the car contest. And you get a tax break for having a baby whereas with the car you have to pay taxes.

Moral of the story: Find people that are willing to come watch movies or read books or just sit on your couch and stare at the wall while your child sleeps so that you can go out and do things after seven. Even if you just use that time to run to the grocery store or go to a movie or get a bite to eat, it is good to get out of the house at night so you don't feel trapped.

Homemade with Love

For those of you who are a bit crafty like me, it is a big deal to make baby blankets for people who are having a baby. And an even bigger deal when the crafty person finishes the project before the intended recipient turns twenty five and no longer needs a baby blanket. Many mothers have tried to make something for their children only to get caught up in life, never to finish the projects they started.

Ada is lucky to have a lot of people who are crafty who love her as she has a collection of homemade blankets. She has one from her Great Grandma Helen (who passed away just a few months before Ada was born, crocheted with a border finished by her great aunt Connie), her Grandma Barb (crocheted), her mom's friend Cassie (knitted), her mom's friend Heather (a quilt with her name and birthday sewn on it), her mom's friend Lorraine (cross stitched), and finally me—her mom (knitted, seen above, and finished before Ada turned seven-months old— which is a big deal for crafty people trying to get things done on time). She also has handmade hats (Amanda, Rebecca, Sherry O), a poncho (Rebecca), sweaters (Sherry O, Barb, me someday hopefully), booties (Cassie, Rebecca), and even a sock elephant with a dress and a bow in her hair (Cassie).

The times when mothers made all of their children's clothes has pretty much passed us by. But I'm proud to say that I was able to knit a blanket for my baby to enjoy as a constant reminder that she is loved. I started it months before she was born and it spent hours draped across the belly that she called home for ten months. Hopefully it will spend many more hours providing her warmth and a sense of security as she grows into a beautiful woman.

Moral of the story: The love that goes into a handmade gift for a baby is unmatched. If you're crafty, consider sharing that love with a little bundle of joy in your life.

A Random Hodgepodge of Thoughts

Being a parent makes you more sensitive to all the tragic crap that goes on in the world. National disasters, sad news about the loss of a child, what it would be like for a child to lose a parent and overall how precious life is. I'm more sensitive to the news and I try to be more aware of other parents, women with strollers, and ways I can be more helpful to new moms. It changes the way you see the world.

Having a child means your world is inundated with toys. Bouncy seats, exerscausers, swings, Boppys, Bumbos, playmats, blocks, stuffed animals, books, etc. Prepare to trip on all of it and get used to having bruises resulting from stumbling.

And speaking of bruising, keep ice packs handy in the freezer for when you happen to bump your head putting the car seat in and out of the car. Or for when the door hits you in the elbow as you try to shimmy through it while wrangling the car seat and the diaper bag and the stroller through at the same time.

Do your best to get your rest. It's tough with kids but take naps when you can and go to bed early every once in awhile just to replenish yourself.

Moral of the story: Try to stay positive, watch where you are going, and get your sleep so you're in the best shape for keeping up with your kid.

Kennel Vs. Bus Locker?

When I removed Ada from daycare after we decided it wasn't working, my father made a comment I will never forget.

Amanda: "I pulled Ada from daycare. It just wasn't working out and she wasn't adjusting to it."
Dad: "Well, that's okay. Sometimes it doesn't work out."
Amanda: "It's just stressful because it is really hard to get into a daycare in the city."
Dad: "You can always put her in a kennel."

After analyzing that statement, it makes perfect sense. I'd pay about the same amount on a daily basis, she'd get groomed, her nails would be clipped, she'd get to play with the other "kids", they'd pick up her poop, she'd be well fed, exercised, and would have plenty of one-on-one attention and time for naps. Not a bad idea.

Then talking to my boss about how daycare wasn't able to spend one-on-one time with her, wanted her to be able to play by herself and be more independent, etc.

Me: "I had to pull Ada out of daycare since it wasn't a good fit for her. They wanted her to play on her own and be an easy baby, nap a lot, entertain herself. My dad said I should just put her in a kennel but that seems to be too expensive."

My boss: "Well, if they aren't going to give her one-on-one attention and interact with her, you might as well put her in one of those storage lockers at the bus station. Aren't they just a quarter? And you could leave her there indefinitely. Just stop by every so often to change her diaper, feed her. That's way cheaper than $100 a day and she'd get the same treatment."

Moral of the story: It's always good to have people in your life who can find the humor in a stressful situation.

July

Who's Gonna Watch My Kid?

Drama Drama Drama...

I think I left off about a week ago saying that Ada was done with daycare, we were off to interview nannies, yada yada yada.

Thanks to help from my friend Colette, we contacted a nanny/caregiver search agency and they sent over three very nice women to interview to be Ada's super nanny. Candidate #1 had no prior experience with infants—even though that was part of what I requested. And boy did we ever look dumb in the interview! My husband and I had no clue what we were doing. We weren't prepared, didn't print out a list of questions and I just kept saying, "Hmmm, what else do we need to ask about. Umm..." Like an absolute moron. Thankfully Rick is better at making stuff up and asked some good conversation questions. Here is a mini list to get you started in case anyone ever has to interview a nanny. I'm told the trick is to sit down and figure out what you want from them beforehand as it is a real help. (Which I did but the printer ran out of ink.)

Nanny Interview Questions

Why do you want to be a nanny?
Are you looking for a full-time or part-time job?
Do you know CPR? First Aid?
Are you willing to do the baby's laundry and dishes?
How do you put a baby down for a nap?
What do you do when she is fussy?
Are you willing to give the baby medicine? What kind?(Prescriptions, over-the-counter, teething gels? For liability some won't do it at all.)
What is your prior experience with infants?
What is your education level? Are you in school? What are you studying?
Are you typically on-time, late, early?
Are you available from 8 A.M.–5 P.M.?
Can you stay fifteen minutes late or a half hour if we're running late?
Will you sing to the baby? Go on walks? Play? Listen to music?
Can you teach her a foreign language?
Can you lift more than thirty pounds?
What will you do with the baby during the day?
What is your hourly rate?
What days can you work? What times?
When are you available to start?
Can you drive? Do you have a car?
Can you baby sit at night occasionally if needed? Weekends?
Do you watch television?
Do you have references we can call?
Do you smoke?
Do you have siblings?
How would you get here? Drive/Public Transit?
How long does it take to get here?
Where do you live?
Will you be supplying your own meals?
Can you swim?
Do you have kids?
And most importantly—watch how the interviewee interacts with the baby and if the baby likes her/him.

As I was saying... Nanny #1 was nice but had no experience and was holding Ada all wrong. The kid was so uncomfortable it was just bad. And her English was mediocre.

Nanny #2 was great. Even though I am really against smoking, she does smoke but never while at work and she didn't smell of smoke. She had experience, good personality and spoke English well.

Nanny #3 was okay. Her experience was with her nephew or something. She was a little late, nervous, and just didn't have any confidence. She is married, lives with her parents, wants kids, wants to go back to school to be a nurse or something... tons of ambition but no backbone to actually do anything about it. That bothered me. Plus I already liked #2.

I called the agency back the next day to report on the interviews —which we scheduled for a half hour each and that was just right. I'd do forty-five minutes each next time just so we aren't rushed in between. We got the references for #2 and she checked out. I called to offer her the job but she had two more interviews for full-time work and we were only offering part-time work so, she'd have to let us know. My gut said she wouldn't pick us so I went to plan B—which I also have to credit Colette with.

Being a member of a million mommy groups did have its advantages. Colette's friend had a niece looking to babysit over the summer. She's a student at Depaul, babysits a ton, has two younger siblings. Great. I contacted her to come over for an interview. If the nanny came through, I'd be able to use her as a night/weekend babysitter as needed. We met and she was really impressive so I hired her on the spot, without my husband. He met her at the end of the interview and liked her too. After she left, I asked him if it was okay that I hired her because I was sure the nanny would fall through and he said "Honey, I trust your judgement."—Straight out of "How to be a good husband and father 101".

I laughed at him and said, "Good answer". The catch with this deal was that this babysitter could only watch Ada two of the three days I needed her. But, she was in a sorority and knew two other people that could do Thursday. Great. So I set up a meeting to meet and train them both the Monday before they started.

They showed up a half hour late. Mind you she was a half hour late for her first interview too but I had been wishy washy about the interview time and said I was free all night and she called to say she lost track of time, just got out of the shower and would be right over. Okay. So she isn't punctual. I know and can prepare for that. Rick and I went through the training stuff. All went well. Her friend was super nice and Ada seemed to like them both. We made plans for them to come at seven forty-five on their given days and they were off on their merry little ways. BUT... before they left, Rick got in a little "Please be on time and if you are running late, be sure to call so we can plan accordingly."

It was Tuesday, seven forty-five in the morning. She was not here yet. Eight. Not yet. Eight ten. Seriously? Eight thirteen the phone rang. "Oh my God, I am sooo sorry. My alarm didn't go off. I am coming over right now." Eight thirty she finally got here and apologized. What could I do? I was forty-five minutes late for work at that point and still needed her to watch my kid. So I decided to deal with it later. I walked to the bus, and waited. Ten minutes passed and I got on the bus. At nine thirty I finally got to work. An hour late at that point, but whatever.

I worked. La te da. La la la. Four thirty I left for the bus. Got to the bus stop. Four forty la la la. I saw a bus. Nope, not my bus. Four forty-five my bus arrived, full, and didn't stop to pickup or drop off any passengers. Hello CTA! I had to be home at five to show my new babysitter what a good example of a punctual person was. This whole bus crap wasn't helping! I waved down a cab and paid $14 to get home. I arrived five minutes late. So much for setting that good example.

Upon getting home, the sitter downloaded Ada's day for me. All went well on day one. Baby was in one piece and alive so the sitter got credit for that. Then I asked, "Are you usually late?" And she says, "Oh no. Never. It's just that the two times I've come to meet with you I was coming from my parents house in the suburbs and miscalculated traffic, and this morning I tried to use my alarm on my palm pilot for the first time and it was confusing..." So I made a few jabs and references to being on time and here by seven forty-five for Wednesday and she assured me she wouldn't be late.

It was Wednesday. Seven forty-five. She should have been here already but that would have been a miracle. Seven fifty. Really? Not again please. Seven fifty-five she pulled up and buzzed the door. Then she proceeded to ask if she needed to move her car because a quarter of it was overlapping with the temporary loading zone. Ug. If she just would have gotten here at seven forty-five like I told her to, there was a nice spot open right across the street. So I suggested she move her car. But we didn't see any spots so I suggested that we drag Ada outside in the car seat so I could set her on the sidewalk as I pulled out of my spot to leave and she could take my spot and then take Ada back inside.

As soon as we got outside, a prime spot opened up, but once the sitter started to pull out, Joe Schmoe took it. We did the car in/out switch and all was well with the world. I went to work, almost hit a guy on his bicycle with my car, and had the parking meter eat a few quarters without giving me credit, but that was all pretty standard for a day in Chicago.

It sounded like today went okay but Ada didn't take an afternoon nap and was pretty fussy. The sitter called at three o'clock for suggestions on how to calm her since she was out of ideas. I suggested milk and that may have worked a bit because it sounds like things got better. I got home and Ada was famished and fussy but still alive and healthy. I'm going to give the sitter another shot next week. Two more days to see how things go and after that, I don't know what I'll do. But I didn't know what I'd do when I pulled her from daycare either.

Moral of the story: Boy scouts know what they are talking about when they say "Be prepared". It comes in handy when interviewing nannies. Be on time, otherwise you tend to look like an idiot. Have faith that things will work out in the end, they usually do—just not always how you'd like them to. And try your best to just go with the flow. You can't control the world so don't stress yourself out trying.

Ada's Sleep Schedule

Someone asked how I got Ada to stop feeding to sleep. So here goes...

I sprinkled her with fairy dust.

No. I just stopped feeding her before putting her in her crib.

She sort of adjusted to it, and then didn't. Her naps were all messed up because she went and played at Grandma's for a weekend after getting pulled out of daycare and now had two new daytime babysitters who were trying to figure out the best way to get her down for her naps.

I must mention that Ada has always been a good sleeper for us and has been sleeping through the night (six or eight hours at a time) since she was ten pounds or so, and really all the way through the night (ten to twelve hours) at about thirteen pounds—experts say that is the "magic number". But she came into this world sleeping four to six hour stints when most kids were up every three hours. She might be a rare breed.

Here's what worked for us so far (sort of)...

At six months, Ada got up around seven, ate (she was on solids), played, went glassy-eyed and slowed down, got a little more fussy, rubbed her eyes against my shoulder when I picked her up and took a forty-five minute or longer nap around nine. Then she ate, played, glossed over again around one and went down for an hour or more. Again, she got up, ate, played, maybe grabbed a cat nap for twenty minutes around five and then was out for the night at six thirty or seven. The trick to getting her to stop feeding right before bed was that we were in an eat, play, eat, sleep routine and I swapped the second eat portion out with a sway, shhhhsh, sing, bounce for a few minutes in front of the crib, then put her down to scream for five to ten minutes as I occupied myself with dishes or other housework to avoid focusing on her screaming. To keep me out of her room while she settled down, we had an egg timer on the fridge and I had to wait for it to hit fifteen minutes before I could go rescue her. If I had to go in, I settled her down for about five minutes and then tried the "cry it out" thing again with the timer. If that failed, I got her and waited until she went glossy-eyed to try again.

Some days it all fell apart. Most of the time it worked well. She was teething now too so if she was having a really bad day and spazzing out so badly I didn't know what to do, I admit that I caved in and nursed her. But then I tried to wake her a bit if she fell asleep, I read her a book or poem and then put her in her crib. Or even changed her diaper one more time in between. Anything to get her to break the eat-to-sleep association.

I also tried not to ever leave the house during nap time. That was just asking for trouble.

Moral of the story: Feeding your kid to sleep is bad (it can rot their teeth and cause ear infections), but sometimes bad things happen to good people. Just try your best and see what works for you and your child. What doesn't work today, might work tomorrow.

Endangered Species: Date Night

Now that we have Ada, Rick and I rarely go out by ourselves. And when I say rarely, I mean that I can sit here and write about each and every time we've gone out without Ada—just the two of us—because the number is very small—four times actually. We went to a movie for Rick's birthday in March—he picked the ever romantic "No Country for Old Men" which I proceeded to rate as the most disturbing movie I've ever seen. Then to our big date back in our hometown that involved a fancy steakhouse, Target and the local custard shop while Grandma Ba watched Ada sleep. For my birthday we went to Indiana Jones and had pizza. And finally dinner at a local restaurant two blocks away while my mom was babysitting Ada.

Sure, we've been to parties and out to dinner with friends, but most of the time we went in the afternoon and took Ada with or one of us stayed home—she's a great excuse for not attending things when we'd really rather stay home—and on rare occasions, we found a sitter.

But not just any sitter, mind you. No. We've done our best to work the system of friends who always offer "Anytime you need a sitter. Just give me a call. I'll gladly come watch her." Unfortunately for those who offered, but actually wanted to play with her to get their baby fix, she went to bed at seven or earlier and they just came to our house and hung out while she slept. It helped that we had a lot of movies, high speed Internet, and encouraged them to bring books along. I just couldn't bring myself to pay someone $10 an hour to sit in my house and read for three hours while we went to grab a bite to eat. It just seemed silly. And so many of our friends didn't mind or at least didn't tell us they were too busy washing their hair.

So my many thanks go out to all of those wonderful friends and family members who offered to help watch Ada. We really appreciated all of them and how they contributed to our sanity. And how they weren't a drain on our wallets.

Moral of the story: When you're ready to have kids, be sure to have a collection of single friends who don't mind getting their baby fix at your house. It does wonders for your sanity, and helps those who just aren't ready to be parents but love kids to fill their baby contact quota. Everyone wins.

"I Want the Pink One!"

Never before have I given much thought to a car seat. Once you have a child, it becomes a big deal. If you get the wrong one, you could be putting the life you worked so hard to bring into this world in danger. You wouldn't want your baby to be in an unsafe car seat would you?

Of course not. So, being the busy mom that I am, I have passed off the process of researching and purchasing Ada's new car seat to none other than my wonderful husband, Rick.

For those of you who have never shopped for car seats before, watch out. What a task. And it isn't something that you just do once and move on. No. It turns out that you have a baby, and then that baby grows, and grows, and grows. And what no one tells you is that it isn't just their cute little clothes that they outgrow. No siree, Bob! They outgrow their strollers and their car seats and their toys and their shoes and everything in between.

So here is car seat 101, albeit abbreviated since I haven't really researched all this stuff myself.

You have a baby, and then you have to have a car seat to take the baby home from the hospital. It will typically fit a newborn up to twenty-two pounds. You should get a little u-shaped padding bumper to go around their tiny heads when you first use it. I got lucky and had a friend with twins, Michelle, who sold me her Graco Snugride—probably the most popular car seat out there. I trusted her judgement and didn't ask questions knowing that she researched everything baby and was now a pro since she had successfully managed to get her twins to age two. Amazing! (Terrifying too!)

Once your child approaches twenty-two pounds—depending on the car seat (sooner for some kids like Ada who are bordering on being Amazonian), you need to get the next size up. Some car seats then go up to thirty-five pounds or fifty-five pounds or whatever, but kids have to be in a car seat until eighty-five pounds or so. (This is all from memory so check my facts and feel free to make note that I am an idiot.) And then you get to buy a third car seat for the last stretch of growth. You lucky duck! Unless you get the second car seat to go from five pounds to eighty-five pounds—which is what Rick suggested.

Okay, so now that we have that out of the way...

My darling Rick started researching, and I starting throwing every link I could at him so he could make an informed decision. He even watched the videos on YouTube of the parents who had lost a child because they picked the wrong type of car seat or were unlucky. Apparently booster seats and seat belt only car seats are bad. Five-point harnesses are the only way to go. And wait to turn the seat forward as long as possible. Facing backwards is best for as long as the seat is designed for it.

After about two weeks of intense research, Rick found the seat of Ada's dreams. The Radian 80. Ohhh, ahhh. He made his decision after carefully weighing the pros and cons. After reading reviews from loving mothers everywhere that daughters adored their pink car seats, Rick was hooked. Ada should have the pink one—the Pink Princess to be exact. Not the grey version that matched our car's interior and would be less obnoxious, but the bright pink one that screamed "girlie".

Fine. Whatever you want honey. After all, she'll be in it until she's several years old so she might as well like it. It isn't like she'll be passing it on to a little brother or anything so who cares if it is pink?

We headed to the store to get the new car seat, and they only had the grey one in stock. And it was the last grey one they had. And it had been open and on display for four days so they were willing to give us 15% off—15% off a $300+ car seat was a big deal. So we quickly said, "Sorry Ada, screw the pink one. We're getting the grey one." Rick was bummed but you could tell he was excited to get the discount. We waited for the guy to find all of the parts for the seat. We tested it out in our car to make sure it fit and it did, sort of—assuming I never sat in the front seat again or that I enjoyed having my knees at my chin for long car rides. And then the guy came back to say, "We don't have the bumpers that go around her head in stock. We must have given them away with the last car seat so I'll order them and they'll be in next week. I'll give you 25% off and call you when they come in."

"SOLD!" Rick replied.

Sorry Ada. It just wasn't meant to be.

While the sun shone brightly on us (or not-so-bright-pinkly), our neighbor Colette wasn't fairing so well. She had the Orbit travel system that her husband thought was "so cool" and was now less than excited about after learning that the handy dandy "system" just meant she had to buy three car seats over the growth of little Eva as the second car seat went up to fifty-five pounds and she would need the third one after that. The second one had been on back order for about a month and she finally got one after paying a premium and getting aggressive about tracking it down. And she found out that she has to buy a separate seat to attach to the stroller or Eva would be sitting straight as a board as they strolled the neighborhood. In the end, the travel system cost her the travel budget!

Here are a few tips and things to keep in mind when looking for car seats in case you are in the market:

Comfort
Safety Rating
Tilt-ability
Cost
Size—Will it fit in your car? What if you have more kids?
Portability—Is it heavy or awkward? Does it have travel carrying straps or a carrying case?
Does it look cool? (Pink? Grey?)
Are the seat belts easy to adjust?
Think about the color... Black will heat up in the summer.
Wash-ability?

Will it fit in the trunk if your child isn't with you?
Does it have covered metal hooks so kids don't get burned if it
has been in the sun?
Is it compatible with your car? *http://www.carseatdata.org/*

Moral of the story: When it comes to doling out the big dough
for large purchases for baby, do your research and try to plan
ahead.

Stranger Magnet

For some reason, unbeknownst to me and my friend Colette, if
you are out walking with a baby—especially in a baby carrier on
your chest, random people must talk to you. They just can't
resist. I don't know what it is about babies but they make
everyone your friend instantly.

Today for instance, Colette and Eva, Ada and I were out on a
long walk. We started off casually heading to the CVS to pick up
photos. CVS was too busy but while we were in the store, a
woman stopped me to ask about Ada and to tell me about
sunhats back in the day. She said they used to have sunhats
secured with elastic chin straps. As I stood there with my
feelers out for any sign of weirdo-wacko danger, she told me
about how one day her son was wearing one of the hats with the
elastic and he proceeded to grab the strap, pull it far from his
face and then let go of it before she could intercept it from the
painful retraction into his chin and the blood curdling scream
that followed. Poor kid. Thank goodness for Velcro and snaps
that we have nowadays.

Then we saw a guy playing a guitar. He told us his kid was a
teenager now and then said something about how it is
important, once the babies start standing up, that we read to
them. We assured him we already read to them and continued
on our way.

As we rounded the next corner, a middle age gentlemen was
walking the same direction as we were and said "Is that carrier
comfortable?"
To which I replied. "Yeah, it's not bad. I've only had it a few
weeks but it is an Ergo designed to be good for the back. I have
a few herniated discs in my neck and so I try to be careful as

much as I can." He walked with us about a hundred feet toward his place and explained that he is always mindful of his posture as he has had back surgery and has a cage in his spine or something that sounded painful. But he was very nice.

Then, near the bike path on Lake Shore Drive, a car didn't wait for us at the crosswalk and a woman proceeded to tell us how you always have to watch for them because they are unsafe. Then she gave us a lesson on watching for bikers on the path because they will run you over as they are going too fast and being so unsafe.

And just the other day when we were out walking, another random guy asked us if it was weird that we once had the babies in our bellies and now we wear them on our chests. We told him we hadn't really thought about it but that is an interesting thought.

So if you are looking for ways to improve your social skills or attract more random people and wackos, just strap a baby to your chest and come for a walk in my neighborhood. It's always a good time.

Moral of the story: Babies attract weird people. Go with the flow, smile, nod and when all else fails, keep walking.

Childcare Update

Okay, so I don't even know what to call the people who watch Ada. Right now it is a "babysitter" because I think "nanny" is more of a professional who does this for a living whereas babysitter is more temporary. Either way, whoever is taking care of my child is only temporary as I found out last week that sitter #2 who comes on Thursday is no longer available, and sitter #1 who comes on Tuesdays and Wednesdays is done as of September tenth when her semester starts back up. So here I am, still juggling the sitter crap. Which again makes me really thankful for my boss and my job and how flexible things are in my life right now because I couldn't do it without that... and I get by with a little help from my friends. Sorry, couldn't resist. But really, I do. I have friends that are willing to cover for me in a bind and that is really helpful since Grandmas Ba and DD are over an hour away.

So what am I on? Plan F at this point? Daycare didn't work, hodge podge grandma coverage was temporary, the nanny interviews failed, sitter one will be okay for a bit, sitter two is done, sitter three comes Friday, so I guess this is Plan G since I know sitter three is temporary because I'm trying to help her find a job in Human Rights here in Chicago. I'm thinking these younger "sitters" aren't taking this as seriously as I'd hoped, which is to be expected since they are "sitters" and not "nannies". At least they are giving me notice instead of dropping the ball completely.

From my experience so far, if I were a nanny/babysitter, I'd only take jobs where the kids are one year or older and aren't sick. It wouldn't be worth it for me to deal with an infant that screams all day because they are teething. I once babysat for a little girl, just a few months old, who had an ear infection and was asthmatic. Her parents had just adopted her and I was shocked that they would leave me with her when she wasn't feeling well. But they did. She screamed the whole time and her older sister kept saying, "This isn't normal; you should call my parents." So I did. I called them about ten times during their movie and they were pissed. Then they went on to tell the other sitters how awful I was because I couldn't handle their baby. I vowed at that moment never to do that to a sitter. And I have a lot of guilt now that Ada is teething because I can't predict when she'll have a screaming fit and when she won't. But at least I leave her sitters with five teething remedies and a good supply of infant Motrin.

Not only can I not get this daytime baby coverage all smoothed out and stress free, but I can't find a sitter for a Saturday night this week. I'm going to have to try *sittercity.com* and let you know how that goes. We'll see.

I still can't complain as I have a friend in Colorado who is having a mess of a time with her sitters and has given up going out altogether until her regular sitter comes back from summer vacation. So it could be much much worse. I'm lucky that I live in a city with great mom groups, many friends, and so much to do. Chicago rocks!

Moral of the story: Childcare can be a never-ending battle so you might as well look for the humor in it all. Learn as you go and hope that your child is learning all of the good things and none of the bad from each person who cares for her.

Splashmat Pee

Following up on my observation that babies are messy—especially since Ada started eating solids—I've been on the hunt for a splashmat or something to protect our rug and floors from her messes. I found a few that were neat. If you want to splurge, one is from Mimi the Sardine and I like that the fabric is recycled or environmentally friendly in some way. But... I wasn't willing to drop $40 on a silly floor mat. I started using a big sheet of plastic but was worried that my little rolley-polley baby would get wrapped up in it. So, I was struck with an idea and bought a vinyl tablecloth from Target for $6 that was enormous and covered half of my living room.

I unwrapped it last night and decided I'd put Ada on it today for some naked baby time—her favorite. Within a minute of me setting her down, she peed on the tablecloth. Then, a few minutes later, she managed to roll herself off near the edge of the mat and peed half on and half off the mat/rug. I still had to clean up the rug, but at least it was only 50% of one pee spot instead of two full pee spots. Better than nothing. Silly kid.

Moral of the story: Creativity can save you a bit of money—not always for the good of the environment but it's good to try—and can help your carpet or rug last a bit longer when you have a baby.

Running the Baby Gauntlet

If you have kids, have babysat for or have visited someone who does, you know what I mean by the "baby gauntlet". Yes, I am referring to all of the crap that somehow turned my home into a dangerous obstacle course.

Heaven forbid the phone rings when you accidentally leave it in the other room as there is no chance of getting to it while avoiding bodily harm from baby stuff.

Say goodbye to straight toes as many a toe has been broken

running the baby gauntlet. And I must say, the bouncy chairs are the worst with their thin wire frames that are perfect for splitting toes and hurting like a *#%$@^! And I thought it was normally tough to stop swearing around the baby but this makes it nearly impossible!

On any given day in our house, I end up bruised and battered by the plethora of baby toys that litter our home. From the exerscaucer, to the bouncy chair, the high chair, the playmat with the dangly things, the swing, the stroller, the car seat—and we aren't even in Ada's room yet!

My house is overrun with her stuff. Her laundry has invaded the bedroom, her diaper pail now occupies the bathroom—in addition to her towel, her rubber duck, and her baby shampoo—she has her own shelf in the kitchen, her own slot for baby spoons in the drawer, and a large portion of the refrigerator and freezer dedicated to storing her milk, jars of baby food, and the ever-elusive teething toys. The hallway is typically strewn with soiled burp cloths as they fall during the chaos of the day, awaiting retrieval when the all clear has been sounded as Ada goes to sleep for the night. A chair in the dining room is dedicated as her high chair, and its parts are usually found scattered across the dining room table, frequently with a slimy bib, wash cloth, and the remnants of her most recent meal crusting over as we overlook putting it away in our haste to serve our new ruling member of the household. The living room floor is her own personal playground with toys that seem to rotate like planes in and out of O'Hare Airport. Outside her bedroom door is the holding area for laundry and items that need to go into her room, but we don't dare open the door whilst she sleeps for fear of waking our little angel. And then there is the area right in front of the front door—a.k.a. where we park the stroller when we are too lazy to move it into the closet or collapse it into the corner until our next adventure out. The only place she hasn't conquered is the hall closet and the back porch—but it's only a matter of time. We're already talking about putting the baby pool on the back porch and I'm sure her towels, lotions and baby oils will soon commandeer the hall closet too.

But at least it's obvious I have a baby. And it's a great way to tell who your true friends are. They are the ones who still come over and don't scowl at you upon entering your baby's new kingdom of chaos. They don't mind that you have stuff everywhere and haven't had much time to pick up, let alone clean for them. And they love you anyway.

Moral of the story: You might bang up a few toes and feel like your home has been invaded. You will likely miss more than a few phone calls due to the hoards of baby stuff cluttering your home. Chances are you'll lose touch with a few friends along the way. But babies are still worth all the chaos.

A Fine Gentleman & Then Some

Ada is a lucky girl. During her seven months here on earth, she's been blessed to get to know a lot of people, but especially her great grandpa. He passed away this week from cancer that finally got the better of him. But he didn't go down without a fight—she gets her stubbornness from him.

Ada's great grandpa was the best there is. He lit up every time we saw him, even though his treatments were draining most of his energy. He still managed to give the best hugs, share the best stories, and make you feel like you were special. His laughter was contagious, his smile bigger than any I've ever seen. And Ada loved sitting on his lap and just staring at him.

She was in awe. He'd smile at her and she'd smile right back in the big open mouth smile that said, "Hey, I like you. I'm not sure what's going, on but this is really fun."

I'm glad they had the chance to spend a little of what time he had left together. After all, that meant I got to spend more time with him too. He will be greatly missed and remembered often.

Moral of the story: Babies are a great excuse to spend more time with the people you love, and the excuse never gets old. Use it often, you won't regret it.

August

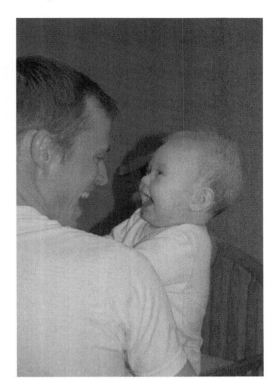

Recovering Slowly

When there is a death in the family, it helps to have a small child accompany you to all of the related events (i.e. visitation, ceremony and funeral). This past weekend was tough for the entire family, but made bearable for me at least, by having Ada with us. I stood in the back of the funeral home during the visitation with her as she cooed and sang, making the only audible sounds at times as everyone in the room reflected on life and death. It was a comfort in a way to know that the circle of life continues—how very <u>Lion King</u> of me, I know.

And at the funeral mass, I was able to hold Ada for the first portion of the ceremony in the church as she was amazed by the three, yes three ceiling fans. That worked for about ten minutes, then the music entertained her for another five minutes and finally, with my mom's help, we moved out to the church's front yard so as not to completely disrupt the rest of the service.

Ada timed her nap well as my mom took her home while I attended the burial. Spending so much time with family causes you to reflect on many things but also to learn a lot about your family. For instance, Ada's great grandma on Rick's side of the family died fairly recently—in 1990. She's the one Ada is named after, even though we didn't really intend to name her after a family member but it just happened that we liked the name. And then it turns out there is a Great Grandma Ada on my side of the family too. Bizarre. I never met either Ada, but Rick attended his Grandma Ada's funeral. Which I found a little weird because after paying our respects to Rick's grandfather, we were led around the tent to see the family resting area—complete with a tombstone with Grandma Ada's name on it—same as my daughter's name. Creepy, but cool at the same time. From the stories told this weekend about Great Grandma Ada, she was a wonderful woman.

On the other hand, my mom's Grandma Ada, whom she never met, was not quite the upstanding citizen we'd have preferred. According to my mom, her Grandma Ada had six kids with her husband and then left him and the kids to run off with another man, leaving the six kids to be split up into foster care—my grandfather being one of them. And the sixth child was questioned as to belonging to her husband or not. Drama! So we are sticking with the story that our Ada is named after Rick's Grandma Ada who was a wonderful person.

And I'll just say, while it was great to have Ada with us for all of the family events, funerals are also a good time to catch cooties... so remember your hand sanitizer. Rick caught a cold and gave it to Ada and now we're listening to the biggest cough from the smallest little thing. To make matters even more exciting, Ada had her first episode of projectile vomit today. Poor thing. Her cough was just too much. We're hoping for a speedy recovery, and some teeth while we're at it.

Moral of the story: Family is always important to stay close to, not just in bad times, but in all times. And a little hand sanitizer can do wonders when you're planning to shake a gazillion hands. Use it often.

Tornado Baby!

Back in the day, when it was just Rick and I, if a tornado siren went off, we'd get excited, stare out the windows and eventually, maybe, take cover under the stairs. But now that we have Ada, protocol has changed. Last Monday night, the sirens went off in the city and we had a debate on our hands. We wondered, "Is this for real? Do we really need to take cover or am I hearing things? Can we just hang out until it sounds like a train is coming and then jump under the stairs?" The problem this time was that Ada was peacefully asleep in her crib and as they say, you never wake a sleeping baby... unless the tornado sirens are going off.

Rick grabbed Ada and hid under the stairs while I grabbed a flashlight, cell phone and checked the weather channel online. Ada just stared at Rick until it was over, then went right back to sleep. Luckily, the tornado threat passed us by.

Moral of the story: Rules should always be made with exceptions, and tornados are always an exception.

Reasons I'm Thankful for a Seven-Month Old

She's always in a good mood in the morning greeting you with a beaming smile.
Her funny hair makes me laugh.
She's really fun to play with.
She's more efficient and effective than a breastpump.
Her smile is highly contagious.
She's big enough to fit in the stroller without the car seat now which lightens my load, or at least makes it less cumbersome.
My biceps are buff from lifting her.
My body is almost pre-baby again and I still have big boobs.
I've met some fabulous people and made several new friends thanks to her.
We spend more time with family.
Seeing her with Rick is priceless.

Seeing my serious father make faces at her is hilarious.
I get to learn a little Spanish and baby sign language—that makes me trilingual right?
I love my new job and the flexibility of it. I get to work twenty-five hours a week and play with Ada the rest.
She gets me out of the house.
She's a great excuse for a messy house.
Sending out her monthly photo updates helps me keep in touch with friends.
She's a great excuse not to do things—"I can't Honey; I'm feeding the baby."
She lets me take a shower while she plays on the floor next to the tub—but not for long.
She gives great hugs.
She only poops once a day, and often when with a sitter.
She cries less often, and sings more often.
Her hum is soothing.
She adds joy and love to my life.
It's entertaining to watch her learn to crawl.
She helps me realize how lucky I am.
She helps me see the bigger picture in life and not get caught up on the small stuff.
She is fun to cuddle with.

Moral of the story: Sometimes you need to list the positives to help put things in perspective and reduce the overwhelmingness of the negatives.

Mini Surprises

In the last few days, I've found myself surprised by things Ada has done. For instance... while I ate my cereal from a square ceramic bowl, I sat on the couch with Ada on my lap and the bowl in my hand. Being the little teething queen that she was, within a few bites of my Cheerios she had pulled the bowl toward her and started gnawing on the corner of the bowl. I doubt it offered much relief but it was entertaining.

Then, silly me, I sat Ada on the couch so I could go get a long-sleeve shirt since the temperature had cooled and the breeze was making me a bit cold. I left her with a good full roll distance to her right and left, and assumed she'd be fine. As I grabbed the shirt from my drawer I heard a thud and a squeal. I sprinted through the house as I chanted "shit, shit, shit" since I knew she managed to fall off the couch. I arrived to find that she had indeed fallen, but had not rolled to either side. She surprised me again by having bounced herself to the front edge of the couch and flipped off of it, landing with her head opposite from where she started. Lucky for me, she landed on a blanket I had left on the floor and she missed the corners of the coffee table hutch by about six inches. Rick said I've now used up my one freebie so I can never leave her alone again. I never intend to. She was very deserving of the nickname "squirmy worm".

Today I was again surprised when I returned from making our lunches in the kitchen while she was on her playmat in her room. Surrounded by toys galore, what did she chose to slobber on but the fabric skirt of the glider's ottoman. Of all things yummy and good in the world, the ottoman was not one of them.

And, after lunch I was changing her diaper on the floor on her pee mat in the living room when I ran to her bedroom for a wipe and new diaper. Moments later I returned to find a five inch curly turd had been neatly expelled and awaited my removal. Lucky for me, again, she didn't have time to roll in it.

Among all of these surprises, the best was learning that Ada loved to bounce, jump, and skip. Or more specifically, she loved it when we held her while bouncing, jumping or skipping. Galloping worked too. The result of our movement was easily the biggest smile in the history of the Universe. Followed closely by the huge smile achieved as we stood her up on the couch to look out the window while enjoying a cool August breeze. This, my friends, was one happy baby—despite all of my negligent mommy moments.

Moral of the story: Don't be lulled into the false sense of security during the first six months. Once these babies go mobile, they need constant supervision. And the surprises never end.

Three Days Away

Ada turns eight-months old tomorrow and I decided this past weekend it was time for me to get some much needed mommy alone time. I pumped like crazy and stocked as much milk as I could manage and took the Megabus to Minneapolis. Yes, the Megabus. I would have flown but since flights were $400, it just wasn't going to happen. Eight hours each way and $50 later, I had a lovely trip to the Twin Cities.

I've only left Ada for about twenty-four hours before so this was a big deal, kinda. I was worried about taking the bus as I typically don't travel well, but it was actually quite nice. And I ran into an old friend on the bus returning home (it's a small world...la la la). Crazy. But I will say, to all you moms out there who haven't taken a break, do it! It was awesome. I missed my husband more than the baby and it was so nice to get to sleep in until ten thirty or eleven in the morning—granted I was staying out until two in the morning and partying like a crazy woman five years my junior but I won't get to do it again anytime soon so what the heck.

What made my weekend so fabulous? Hmmm... Well, I got to wear my friend's cute clothes, have fun girl time, go shopping with no sales tax—major bonus when you lived in Chicago, and oh, yeah, I got to see MC Hammer and Cindy Lauper in concert in a combined fashion show benefit called Glamorama. And they were awesome! Hammer really is too legit to quit. And Cindy's buff. Wow. Very entertaining. I ate well, walked too much—which was good for my attack on the last lingering pounds of baby weight, and probably did more damage to my finances than I cared to admit. But I did get a deal at a garage sale where a woman my size was unloading cute tops for cheap. Eleven tops later, I had to do some creative packing to get home.

While away, I worried about not having enough breast milk for the three days I was gone. I came home just in time the supply ran out the night before I got home and I returned at six thirty to wake Ada up and feed her. Now I just have to get her to eat all of the milk I collected on the trip before it goes bad. Who said motherhood was easy? Milk logistics and management should be a degree.

Moral of the story: Live a little. Don't stress so much about the baby. And go do something for yourself every once in awhile. It does wonders on your dark circles (in theory that is, assuming you actually get some sleep instead of partying like a crazy momma in four inch heels). Oh, and pack some band-aids for all of your new found blister friends.

Put on Your Own Mask First

I joined a new book club this week, made up mostly of moms... and our first book to read was *The Price of Privilege* by Madeline Levine. It was about "How parental pressure and material advantage are creating a generation of disconnected and unhappy kids". The amateur psychologist in me loved reading it. And the mom in me wanted to buy five-hundred copies to pass out to everyone I knew. Not that the book gave concrete solutions on how to parent if you were an affluent family, but it did bring up some key points that I thought were valuable for a mother's self reflection. And a father's too but it was mostly geared to moms.

What was so great about it? Here are the highpoints (Cliffnotes don't cover this kind of thing...) or what I took from the book.

It turns out, parents really can screw up their kids. If they are depressed, absent, mean, etc, it really messes up their kids. Therapy can and does help, but you should get the whole family started ASAP if you are messed up. And most families don't want to admit they are messed up so instead they choose to be miserable and messed up instead of embarrassed and working on getting un-messed up. Funny how that is. However, whether you are a working mom or a stay-at-home mom doesn't seem to correlate with how messed up your kids are.

According to the book, we are all a mirror of our parents— imagine that. But really, I like to help others because that's what my mom taught me was the right thing to do. But it also works in reverse. If you are a jackass to others, your kids will be rude jackasses too. And the rest of the world won't thank you for that later.

All ages are important for kids developmentally, but ages twelve to eighteen are key in an adolescent's life since that is when they need to find a sense of self and what they like/dislike, etc. That is not the time to say, "I'm a doctor so Johnny is going to be a doctor too." And really not the time to say, "Susie, I think you need a boob job and some lipo so that you can run with the popular crowd, oh, and here's a new Porche for turning sixteen." It isn't the time to demand perfect grades or steer your kid to be captain of the football team when he wants to play the lead in Oklahoma. No wonder kids these days are completely messed up. Hello! Where's Captain Obvious when you need him?

As parents, we also need to be positive and supportive. Not critical, judgmental and overbearing. Involved is good, but over involved is bad. Setting limits and rules is good, as well as enforcing them consistently. Balance. Kids need space and privacy, but not aloof parents who leave them home alone for a weekend—and then act shocked when the kids throw a huge keg party and the parents get a collect call from jail while sunning in the Caymans. Uh, duh. Hire a responsible sitter you moron.

(Some of the stories she tells are so obvious—or should be—but some parents these days really don't get it.)

What I also like about it is that she says you should NEVER let your kids buy their way out of trouble. And I completely agree. Her kid once had a drinking party that got busted while she was upstairs sleeping and she made her son go to court and testify that the charges against her should be dropped. He and his friends cleaned up the house, he missed several basketball games, attended all lawyer meetings, paid lawyer fees, and all in all, she taught him a real lesson and part of his punishment was dealing with the consequences of his actions. Love it.

She also explains three types of parenting styles—because I said so, I want to be your best friend, and the authoritative warm parent who is loving but also sets limits. My dad was the first, my mom the second, and Rick's parents were the third. No wonder he and his siblings turned out as good as they did. Not only did his parents pick the best of the three styles, but they both did it. And surprise surprise, you and your spouse really need to be on the same page with how you parent.

And finally, my favorite part of the book is the last chapter where she talks about how important it is, as they say on airlines, to put on your own mask before assisting your children with theirs. We moms need to take care of ourselves and make sure that we are setting good examples for our children, leading balanced lives so we are available to them when they need us, and modeling healthy relationships to ensure that we don't set them up for messed up lives of their own. She makes a point to say she understands all that moms are dealing with and juggling and it is hard to keep up appearances when you are doing so much. Just try your best to stay balanced and it will all work out.

Moral of the story: It's a good book, parents make all the difference in the world, and hopefully this book will help them realize how much impact they have on their kids' lives and encourage them to seek help instead of trying to save face if they can't manage—after all, seeing a therapist is a lot better than having a kid hurt himself or someone else.

Another Nanny Update? Geesh!

Yes, it was true. We were still playing the nanny game. Today I interviewed nannies. I found them all on *Sittercity.com* and a few of them actually called me to get interviews which at first seemed weird, but then I found it to be very convenient. And they were persistent which I like.

The first candidate was Gosia. She was Polish, forty years old, very nice. And she was on time. She didn't claim to smoke, drink or do drugs. She couldn't swim—which made me nervous near the lake... but Ada seemed okay with her. She had done this before a few times and asked really good questions about paid holidays, sick days, and if this was a permanent gig or not. So that was all good. And she was available Wednesday as a trial day and then the next week for sure. She was the front runner but I had two more to go.

Unfortunately for her, she arrived while I was on the phone with my friend Anne. My neighbor Kelly was chatting with me in the hallway as she let Gosia in. And my house was a mess as I had high expectations of mopping the floors and getting the ironing done that morning. Which I actually did do, but I hadn't had a chance to put the table and chairs back where they go so I was doing that during the first few minutes of our interview. Oh, and my bras were in the wash so that made things awkward. For me anyway...

The second nanny never showed. The third nanny called to cancel and said she had accepted another job. And the fourth nanny, who started all of this by calling me first to get an interview, called the previous Saturday to cancel since she got another job. One out of four wasn't bad right? At least the nanny I did interview was good. I called to offer her a job for Wednesday as a trial day and if she liked us, we could talk Wednesday night about the full time gig.

I'm sure this won't be the end of the child care saga.

I think pharmaceutical companies who make birth control should print this in their ads to get more business since securing reliable childcare is not part of every future parent's dream.

Moral of the story: It is tough finding someone you trust to watch your child, but there are many different ways to do so. Just do your best to find one you are comfortable with.

September

Can I Keep Him?

Ah, Labor Day Weekend. What better way to spend four days off work than with family right? And with family comes, yep, you guessed it, family pets. Ah, the sweet smell of vacation...and pets.

I must explain here that our parents both have pets and always have. It's something Rick and I feel strongly against as we've always either been allergic or just didn't want to put that much effort into dealing with a pet. Before I grew old and cynical, I was a huge animal lover. Oh the hours I whined to my father while lobbying for a cat. He'd insist his allergies couldn't handle a cat—which he has since proven as he tends to have great sneezing fits shortly after hanging out with the furry fuzzballs— but I kept trying. We had a dog and he was as close as you get to the devil reincarnated. We didn't know how to train him and weren't the best pet owners in the world either. So, after a few bad experiences as a kid, and all the tears that came with a pet passing, I swore off ever having one. I realized how much pets can eat, destroy, poop, and pee. They also shed, get old, can be mean, jump on me, etc., and I decided that I like them more from a distance. Ada was just going to have to deal with that.

It turns out that Ada really loved playing with Rick's parents' four cats. She spent about an hour watching the cats check her out as she sat on the living room floor and had a good time catching their tails and trying to eat them as the afternoon went by. Some of the cats found her to be entertaining while others didn't really care for her at all. But for the most part, her cat encounter was a success. I was not sure if her rubbing her eyes was due to over excitement and sleep deprivation or allergies, but I chalked it up to the former in hopes that she didn't develop the latter.

Then we were off to my parents' house where they had two dogs. Long haired, furry golden retrievers. One old, one young. Both insanely furry. My mom admits that she isn't the best housekeeper so there was quite a bit of fur for Ada to get into. Upon our arrival, Ada quickly made friends with my brother's dog, the youngster, and tried to eat her tail. Then the dog sat on Ada's little lap and that got a laugh. The rest of our stay I was busy pulling fur from Ada's mouth, off her sippy cup, out of her food bowl, and wiping it from her burp cloths and Onesies. One could argue it was an interesting source of fiber or protein or whatever but I would disagree.

Moral of the story: Pets are a lot of things to a lot of people. To me, they are more furry and frustrating than fun and fabulous.

But if the baby likes them, she can visit them all she wants—as long as we can always give them back.

Daycare Nanny Drama Part XXIV

As I've finally learned, this whole nanny/daycare drama is almost never ending. At least until Ada is old enough to stay home by herself anyway. My mom's words of encouragement most recently were, "The best days of my life were not having to buy diapers for you and your brother, and the day I didn't have to find another sitter to watch you guys." So true. Only eight months into Ada's little life and I completely understand.

Here's the latest. We hired a sitter. She came for a trial day. She called at noon to say she couldn't get Ada to sleep. I gave her a few things to try. She called again at one forty-five to say still no nap. Ada should have been down twice that day and she had already had a dose of Motrin for her teeth so the fact that she wasn't napping was a bit crazy. I was home by two and the sitter was done. Ada was really happy to see me. She just didn't like the woman at all. I get that. We can't all get along all the time.

Following my gut, I had a backup sitter waiting in the wings. She came and is currently watching Ada until we can go back through the process and find a more permanent solution. This current woman has a bad back, needs time off for this, that, and something else, and really just doesn't know what she wants to do in life since she got laid off a few months back and is just trying to figure things out. She's not serious about being a nanny and it shows. But Ada seems to like her okay and it's a good finger in the dam for a few weeks.

So, yep, we're back to the drawing board. Luckily I joined *Sittercity.com* a few weeks back and this will be my third time posting this position online. I received two good applications right after posting the opportunity so that's encouraging. But Rick will be doing the interviews and I'll be taking the support role as I just get too emotionally attached to these people and want to help everyone out. It's tough.

My new list of advice is as follows: Make your husband deal with it. All of it.

Moral of the story: The drama won't end, so you just have to learn to accept it and deal with it as best you can. Try to go with the flow and always trust your gut. It will all work out in the end so just have a little faith.

We've Created a Monster!

I always heard, "She'll be walking in no time." "She'll crawl backwards before she crawls forward." "They grow up so fast." "She'll lose all that baby weight once she starts moving," and similar lines. I just shrugged them off and said, "Whatever, I've heard that before. Blah, blahbitty, blah." But now I said it myself and actually understood what it all meant. Heck, my kid already started to crawl backwards! AHHHH! We used to think we had months to baby proof the house and now we have realized we were too late. Gone were the days where we didn't strap her into everything. Gone were the days where we could leave her unattended for five seconds while we threw out a diaper or washed our hands or answered the door. Gone. All gone.

Just the other day I put Ada on the center of her vinyl tablecloth/playmat/rug saver and went to the kitchen and quickly washed her bottles in the sink. Not five minutes later I returned to see that she had somehow worked her little body under the dining room table about six feet from where she started. I even put the boppy and another playmat behind her in case she fell over. She managed to move from a seated position, onto her belly, and then scooted backwards six feet. All of this while she cooed away, happy as can be, assuring me that everything was going well in the living room and I didn't have to worry about her. And yesterday I found her sitting up in the middle of the playmat after I had left her on her tummy while I went to empty her diaper pail. Thirty seconds or less and she was sitting up playing with her toys. What have we done? How did this happen? We've created a monster. Now she was close to crawling, walking and getting into everything.

Even scarier than that, we went to a two-year-old's birthday party this past weekend and saw kids I didn't see on a regular basis. One was eighteen-months old, one just turned two, and another one was four-years old. What a reality check. I mean, I saw my niece every few weeks and was amazed at how she was growing but it was gradual. Then I saw several of our friends' kids and they were growing into perfect, adorable little women and I was a little freaked out. Really. I created a little person. She'll soon be walking and talking and throwing water from the pool on people at the party. Whew. That was a big realization for me. Hello reality.

Moral of the story: Babies eventually grow into real little people, and eventually big people. That's how it works. And I don't think anyone or anything can ever really prepare you for that fact. Good luck.

Bathtime Take Two!

Lately, feeding Ada hasn't gone as smoothly as I'd like it to. Rick was the real pro as he was able to pin her little arms down under the highchair tray without her really noticing. I was able to do that for a little while but she was on to our tricks and wasn't having any of it. Her hands were set free and boy did she ever know how to make a mess!

Last night as I was feeding her an array of pureed fruits and vegetables, she decided she wanted to eat them and wear them and heck, I needed to wear them too. After a short battle to get most of the food into her mouth, I was finally forced to give up and grab her wash cloth. After three trips to the sink to rinse and re-wipe her, she was still filthy. Desperate times called for desperate measures and I was desperate. She had rice cereal in her hair, ears, up her nose, on her thighs, on my forearms, and covering both her tiny hands. She was a complete mess. I held her at arm's-length while I rushed her to the tub hoping that I wouldn't need to shower before bed. She got a nice little bath. I toweled her off, covered her with lotion and was retrieving her new diaper when she decided to roll over on her mat and play a bit. By the time I had the diaper ready, she had peed all over herself, the mat, and then decided to squirm in her new-found puddle. That was the reason for bath number two. Again, at arm's-length I rushed her into the tub for a quick rinse. I toweled her dry, diapered her first this time, then applied lotion. I then dragged all of the pee-soaked tiles from her playmat to the tub for a quick rinse and finally got her to bed. At that point, she was overtired and screamed her little head off for a few minutes to get into the sleep mood and some how it was my fault that she needed not one, but two baths and that she rolled in her pee and threw food all over herself. Go figure. Moral of the story: No matter what you do or how hard you try, the baby will win the majority of the time. Do your best to roll with it and laugh along the way.

Napless Baby

Last weekend was a bit weird for our family when it came to getting much sleep. Ada decided she wasn't going to take naps as she normally did, and that threw us all off. We also crammed a lot into one weekend—cards and dinner with friends, nanny interviews, lunch with more friends, lunch with family and a two-hour drive on each end of it, brunch with other friends, a long walk including shoe shopping, some yoga and even a bit of the Bears game on our snow-covered TV with crummy rabbit ear reception. I guess that was a lot of eating—and amazingly we missed dinner Saturday night as we both crashed at seven for a "nap" that took us through the night until five in the morning. Hmmmm...

Part of the reason for the lack of schedule was Ada teething, and the other theory was that she really wanted to take one big nap nowadays instead of two. I was not seeing how this was going to work out but we would see. She was pretty good on Friday as far as naps went, but Saturday she skipped the afternoon nap to meet the nanny candidates—we interviewed two and liked them both. Hopefully we would secure one of them soon. But boy was that a reason for me to lose sleep. Anyone who thinks finding a nanny isn't stressful is nuts. After Ada fussed the four times we tried to get her to take a nap, I finally broke down and we went out for a two-hour walk. She napped for twenty minutes. It turned out she wasn't much of a stroller napper. She slept well overnight, but was up at five. After drinking and playing in our bed for a bit, Rick finally got her back into bed at seven thirty for an hour-and-a-half morning nap.

She enjoyed a celebratory brunch with friends who got engaged oh, about eight months ago... and really loved sucking on and biting the spoon. When one dropped, she was lucky to have it quickly substituted with another as there were ten of us at the table and plenty of clean spoons to go around. Then, for the drive out west two hours, we had to first refill her tank with milk and do the ever so fun diaper change in the front seat of our tiny Civic with her on my lap while daddy did the quick change. On the road to Oregon, Illinois, she didn't sleep at all and finally had a major breakdown fifteen minutes from our destination. We stopped for a quick feeding that turned into a fifteen minute glug fest followed by intense screaming when it was time to get back into the car seat. Since my bag of tricks was empty, the remainder of the trip was less than pleasant. Upon arriving, Ada was fussy, mommy was crabby, daddy was glad to have a big beer, and after feeding, changing, rocking, and cuddling Ada, she finally took a forty-five minute nap.

As the sun started dropping on the horizon, we loaded up for the ride home. To people who say you just stick a baby in the car and poof they pass out—you lie! My kid doesn't like to sleep in the car. At most she'll give us a half hour stint but in the four hours we were driving this weekend, she didn't give us five minutes. Frustrating.

And speaking of the little angel, it was nine on Monday and she was finally deciding she should maybe get up. She didn't go down until eight last night but that was the last we heard of her. Thirteen hours ago! Yep, we had a real sleeper. Thank goodness.

Moral of the story: Cross your fingers for a good sleeper if you plan to have kids, and do everything you can to help make their sleep schedule work. You'll have a much happier baby in the long run.

Staying Dry on a Rainy Monday

Yes, a rainy Monday. Not only a tough start to a new week, but a rainy one at that. What better thing to do on a rainy day than walk to the zoo for lunch with a friend? At the onset of today's adventure, Ada and I started out dry. She had a fresh diaper and I was showered and ready to start the day. The sun was hiding behind the clouds and the rain hadn't found its way to our neck of the woods just yet. And so our adventure began. With Ada strapped on the front of my chest in her Ergo carrier, snug as a bug in a rug as they say, we set off to the Lincoln Park

Zoo. Not to really go see the animals or anything like that but we had a friend that worked at the Zoo and today was slated for our semi-annual lunch date. I debated taking the bus, but kept missing it as was typically my luck, and opted for the nice stroll instead. We walked the bus route just in case I got tired or the walk took longer than expected. About half way there, I noticed a familiar face—this happened to me a lot so it wasn't much of a shock. It was a woman pushing a stroller and I of course had to see if it really was someone I knew or not.
So I asked, "Is your name Allison by chance?"
And she replied, "Yeah, and you're Amanda right?"

Sure enough, this was a woman I used to have in my business classes at Iowa. She was my roommate's neighbor freshman year and I had known her about seven years ago for about three years. As it turned out, she was an attorney here in the city. Go figure. The weirdest part was that she wasn't pushing her daughter in the stroller, but was watching her friend's daughter, and didn't even live in the neighborhood. What were the odds of that? Pretty good in my world.

So as we were catching up on old times and saying our goodbyes, it started to sprinkle. I popped out my handy dandy trusty umbrella—the one I got for high school graduation and just sent in for a replacement since Totes offered a lifetime warranty—and we continued on our way through the sprinkles.

On the way from the zoo with our friend Ellen, it started to pour, and continued to do so through lunch. For the trip home, we considered taking the bus, but it sped past us as we were walking out of the restaurant. We started walking and Ada fell asleep on my chest. About five blocks into the walk, I was tempted by another bus, but decided the fresh air and exercise would do us both good. So we walked, and walked and walked, through big puddles and small. All the while shifting the weight of the umbrella and my shoulder bag from one side to the other. Finally, about half an hour later, we arrived home. A bit wet and tired, but happy all the same.

Our little umbrella kept us mostly dry...and reminded me that I should probably invest in a few larger umbrellas if we planned to walk together in the rain often as the tiny one just didn't cover as much as it needed to. Once we got inside, I started to change Ada since her socks and lower pant legs were a bit wet.

As I took off her pants and started switching out her diaper, she peed all over everything. Normally when she pulled that trick, she just peed and it went underneath her. Not this time. She waited until I was lifting her legs into the air to situate the new diaper so that when she peed, it went up and back over her hip to soak her shirt and her pants and her back and the changing table and the new diaper and the new diaper cover. Tricky little thing. She was always coming up with something new to keep me on my toes.

Moral of the story: Sometimes even a big umbrella can't save you from getting wet.

Anybody Home?

Today was our new new new new new new new nanny's first day. Her name was Ashley, similar to our sitter two sitters ago. And she was very nice. She was on time, asked a ton of great questions, and was willing to work with the whole cloth diaper thing. She even turned on the oven for Rick since he prepared a roast for some friends for dinner—we've resorted to bribing some sitters with really good food instead of payment. And she didn't call me several times during the day to say she couldn't get Ada to nap or stop crying. So, they had a great day as far as I was concerned.

But... you can imagine my surprise when I walked in just after five and no one was home. The lights were on. The stroller and diaper bag were gone. The house keys were gone. No baby. No Ashley. Nada. Being the calm, collected mother I had chosen to be, I didn't panic. Instead, I went through the list of what ifs... What if they were having fun in the park and lost track of time? What if the new nanny ran off with my kid? What if Ada got hurt? What if Ashley got hurt? What if I didn't tell Ashley I'd be home at five?

So what did I do? I called Rick and said, "Nobody's home."
He said, "Really?" and chuckled a bit.
I explained and said, "Can you give me Ashley's number so I can call and see where she is?"

Now right here, all of you out there should be like "WHAT? Amanda didn't get this girl's name, number, address, cell phone, shoe size, underwear size, coffee preference, references, date of birth, social security number, last five boyfriends (or girlfriends) names and numbers, and have a background check run on her to make sure she wasn't a crazed lunatic or sex offender?" To be honest, no. I didn't. The thought did cross my mind, but because I'm a trusting person and I trusted my gut, I didn't. But I did smack my head when I got home and thought, "What the heck would I tell the police if Ada was abducted?" "Well officer, you see, I, um, found her on the Internet, and um, her name is Ashley, and I think she lives near Halsted and Belmont, or is it Clark and Belmont, and um, she has brown hair, is about my height, maybe a little shorter, and um..." Needless to say, I would have her fill out her life history as soon as I found her.

I was on the phone with Rick and he tried to give me her number, "773— garble garble garble". The line went dead. I tried again. "Hello, Rick, Hello." Cell phone reception cut out again. I called him back. Nothing. Then I started getting frustrated and rose to the next level of worry. Not elevated to Orange or Red like homeland security, but an orange shade of yellow. I forcefully sat my phone on the kitchen counter and grabbed the house phone. I called Rick again and he read me the rest of her number. I called her, and got her voicemail. I left a message to call me back. Then I called Rick and said, "Double check the number because the voicemail was generic." So he did, and it was correct. Then I looked out the front door, and the back door, and the front door again. No sign of them. Hmmmm... What did I do now? Brrrrrrring. The phone rang. "Hey Amanda, I'm at Panera just finishing dinner. I thought you get home at six."
And I thought to myself, "Silly mommy! You forgot to tell her you come home at five every night." Crisis averted.

Moral of the story: Maybe, it might kinda, potentially, sort of be a good idea to get some personal information about the people you leave your kids with in case you ever need it. Maybe.

Nanny Day Two

Yesterday went super duper well for the new nanny Ashley who had an easy day with Ada—minus the cloth diapers and the fact that Ada pooped three times in the morning to the point where

Ashley gave up and decided to try the cloth diapers again another day. She did, however, note that Ada was the "Happiest baby I've ever seen" when she first got here in the morning as Ada was playing and smiling and being silly, as per usual. Ashley even got her to take two one-hour naps and managed to get the stroller in and out of the inner and outer vestibule doors, without locking herself out. Something I considered to be a miracle.

I was both comforted and a bit peeved when I went to hug Ada goodbye in the morning and she quickly turned back to Ashley and reached out for the pass off. She had been doing that a lot lately. She must have been secure in our relationship or bored with me (more likely) since she tended to reach out to go to other people when I was holding her. I was proud of that fact since most babies nuzzled into mom's shoulder and acted shy. Not my Ada. You wanted her, you got her. She even played the same game between Rick and I and we played pass the baby, back and forth, back and forth.

Today, however, wasn't so easy. Ada continued to teethe. I warned Ashley before I left and listed off the twelve steps we took to make her happier when her teeth hurt. "When all else fails, go outside and she'll quiet down," were my parting words of wisdom. I was shocked upon my return, at five not six, to hear that Ada was a fussy little mess all day. Ashley had to resort to drugs twice and got the pleasure of listening to my little fuss pot all day go on and on about her teeth. Ada even whined while outside in her stroller on a walk—very rare for this kid. Talk about making me into a liar on day two. And the result—still no teeth. Someday, sometime, hopefully in the immediate near future, I'll be able to include a photo of this damn elusive tooth (and my very own grin as it will be one of the most glorious days of my life, and Rick's and Ada's too).

Moral of the story: Don't make promises when it comes to the behavior of a nine-month old. She'll sell you out and prove you wrong every time.

Don't I Get Some Kind of Award?

We made it nine whole months! Ada was still alive (and sleeping like an angel), growing like bamboo (much faster than a weed grew), and didn't quite have any teeth yet but they were coming. There was still plenty of time for all that. I still had my sanity, (for the most part)—meaning I was not in a padded cell yet so I took that as a win. Hooray!

Man how time has flown. My friend Cadence pointed out to me that Ada has been out of the womb almost as long as she was in the womb. That was crazy to think about. And it reminded me to count my blessings that I was not having Irish twins since I was not pregnant and didn't plan to be magically having a baby next month. Hooray to that!

A lot changed in the past nine months. I became a mom and that was kind of a big deal. I loved my husband even more than ever because he was an awesome dad, super supportive of me and the things I did and my new role as a mom—minus the whole lack of taking pictures of me and the baby but that was an almost universal issue with men and their baby mommas—and I realized I could not possibly have picked a better partner to have on my family "team" for the next seventy plus years.

Hmmm… What else… I was in a new job that I liked a lot more than my old job. It was really challenging and cerebral which frustrated me but it was great for my career growth. How could I complain when I got to work three days a week and played with Ada four days a week? I couldn't.

With all of these good changes in life, I didn't need no stinkin' award. Ada was plenty reward for me.

Moral of the story: Life is good. Enjoy what you've got. Accentuate the positives. Breathe. Live.

Handy Dandy Hand-Me-Downs

I will say, I am a HUGE fan of the hand-me-downs! Yea, ha! Speaking of which… I need to tell my mom and mother-in-law to hold off on shopping for a bit… hmmm…

My friend and neighbor Colette (mother of Eva who is ten-days younger than Ada and equally big for her age), who just happens to be AWESOME in a million different ways, was reading a mom post from one of the mom networks we belong to and someone was looking to dump off a bunch of nine to twenty-four month girl clothes to a loving family. Super mom Colette was the first to respond and secured the stuff. Not only was that cool, she was willing to split the stuff between Ada and Eva. I ended up doing nothing and made out with a ton of clothes for Ada. Sweet deal if you ask me. I owed Colette big for this and many other things she has done for me.

Not knowing what these hand-me-downs would include, Colette ventured up north for the pick up. It turned out, that was the mother load (pun intended). FOUR garbage bags FULL of clothes! JACKPOT! She called me over to divvy up the loot and we had a blast going through all of the stuff. It was adorable and in great shape, and fun to go through and pick what each of our girls would look good in. Eva had dark hair with the cutest little curls starting to form around her ears and Ada was a light-blue-eyed blond so they each looked good in different colors. This woman had shoes and socks and coats and hats and dresses and skirts and leggings and shirts and halter tops and pajamas and on and on and on. We had to take a break for dinner and go back later to finish sorting through our treasure. It was a major score.

This was just one reason why Colette rocks. She has made my job of being a mom so much easier by being an ear to talk off, a walking buddy to slim the baby belly, a great support in the nanny search, a wise advisor in the ways of child rearing, a good laugh when I needed one, a fellow mother of an Amazonian baby making me feel less "off the charts" with Ada, a reason to get ice cream or chocolate or both, a benchmark for good mothering, and a fabulous friend. I couldn't ask for more and I will be devastated when she moves to Seattle next year for her husband's job (sob sob). I still have about nine months before she moves so I'm going to make the best of it and get as many playdates and walks and chit chats in as I can. Oh, and I'm taking applications for her replacement to start next July. She doesn't have big feet but these are some really big shoes to fill. Clown shoes even. She's pretty funny. We might just have to get that video phone thing set up so we can chat on Seattle time. Unfortunately the whole idea of the girls growing up chatting on "phones" made from empty soup cans connected by string from back porch to back porch won't work once they move. But I hear Seattle is a great place to vacation so she's not going to get rid of us that easily.

Moral of the story: Fellow moms are worth their baby's weight in gold, and then some. (Eva's twenty-three pounds too!)

Nine Month Doctoress Appointment

What was more awful than giving your little one shots? It turned out, it was getting blood drawn.

Poor little Ada had to have blood work done for her nine-month checkup. No shots. Just a check for lead and a blood count. The lab tech put the tourniquet on her little arm and she started wailing. My heart ripped in half. Then, she couldn't get a good vein to pop up so we switched sides and she started all over again. The tech in training also had to feel the vein before they poked Ada with the big mean needle. Then (oh yeah, it kept going) they filled the first vial, then the second. Finally the tourniquet came off and her wails slowed to sobs. Her little tears made her eye lashes clump together and her eyes glistened. Her face turned funny shades of red and purple. I saw all the way down her throat to the depths of her littleness as she opened her mouth in the loudest scream something that small could possibly utter. It lasted only a minute or two but seemed to last forever as her chest puffed up and she gasped for more air to let out the next wail to deliver blow after heart-wrenching blow against all things good, warm and fuzzy about being a mom. Once the needle was out I quickly pinned down the gauze and scooped her up into my arms before the tech could even get the band-aid ready. I went deaf momentarily as she squealed. The tech was too happy to stick the bandage on and bolt out the door never to been seen again. I gave Ada the sign language sign for "all done", quickly opened the door, gathered our things and got the heck out of there. It was traumatic for us both.

She was fine.

She was off the charts for weight at twenty-three pounds, three ounces. She was almost off the chart for height at twenty-eight-and-three-quarters inches long. And she was adorable. That was all the doctoress had to say. That and it was normal for her to walk before she crawled—if that was what she decided to do. And that it was also normal for girls to be walking at nine months, and to have some teeth. She was still working on both at that point.

To celebrate the morning's success, we walked next door to Carter's and got Ada a new Onesie that said "Daddy loves me" to replace the one she outgrew since it was 50% off. Then we got smacked in the butt by the 10.25% sales tax on the way out the door. Thanks Chicago. We followed that with the usual eat, play, sleep, poop, repeat, routine until about four when we experienced quite a treat. Colette and Eva from next door came over for an official playdate complete with music, toys, and (unfortunately) water for the moms (Colette—we really need to work on this for next time and introduce a little bit of vino or something since you do live next door). Colette and I were chatting away with the babes surrounded by toys when all of a sudden, Eva started busting out her new moves. She could crawl! Her little butt whipped down to all fours and started trekking across Ada's play mat and my jaw hit the floor. "What the?" "How did that happen?" Mind you, I saw these two ladies on Friday, just three days ago, and didn't see a hint of this action. Colette's response, "It just did. I don't know. Crazy isn't it." Then, once I had recovered from my awe of the moment, Eva busted out smooth move number two. She magically moved from a roll into a crawl. And this wasn't some wussy crawl. This was an all out, trucking across the room with a toy in one had and a grin from ear to ear. "Attention: She's mobile." "Crap. We're screwed."

Stay tuned. Ada's day is just around the corner. She's a ticking time bomb waiting to blow. Wish us luck.

Moral of the story: Be strong whenever you visit the doctor and just expect that your kid will scream bloody murder at some point during the visit. This too shall pass.

New Job Titles for Mommy & Daddy

Rick and I came to the realization this weekend that our world now revolved around Ada. Spending two days with both sets of grandparents made that very clear. Our new job titles included...

Travel Coordinator

Secure seating (car seat mainly), pack and load luggage, maintain vehicles, confirm flights, pack plenty of necessities, provide snacks, drive, stop for frequent diaper changes and feedings, shade eyes from the sun, maintain proper interior temperature, play baby-friendly music, avoid bumps in the road, and shut up if and when baby wants to nap en route. Guard the car and don't move baby once final destination has been reached if baby is resting.

(Rick is the official Chauffeur but I fill in when he isn't available or is under the influence.)

Wardrobe Crew/Fashion Advisor

Provide multiple wardrobe changes depending on temperature, mood, messiness of eating, change in event, etc. Must remember to include tops, bottoms, hats, shoes, socks, diapers, bibs, and additional coordinating accessories. Wash, dry, fold, hang and iron wardrobe as necessary. Maintain collection of seasonal items in the proper sizes and secure collection for next season and size anticipating needs (all while avoiding the inconsistent brand labeling system that doesn't really correlate to what size baby actually is.)

Personal Assistant/Event Planner

Make sure Grandparents clear calendars to allow for plenty of playtime, cuddles, and meals.
Ensure that cousin Ana is available for playdates.
Arrange for various pets to let baby eat their fur, pull their ears and attempt to ride them without malicious retaliation.
Organize social calendar to maximize party opportunities.
Purchase gifts for said events, wrap them appropriately and sign cards with baby's name.
Schedule daily walks and outdoor activities for fresh air and exercise.
Have swings, exersaucers and playpens available at all potential locations.
Plan parties, birthday celebrations, and neighborhood playdates.

Entertainer

Lug plenty of toys everywhere we go. Make them dance, sing and move on command. Don't forget teething toys, books, music, blankets, etc. When that all fails, always have a back up bottle ready for immediate consumption.

Photographer/Paparazzi

Always carry at least one camera. Supply plenty of memory cards. Charge batteries frequently. Maintain a secondary camera as backup. And prepare to take video as needed.

Historian

Maintain records of "Firsts". Document special events and daily milestones through scrapbooks.

Communications Director

Maintain database of friends, family, babysitters, and neighbors. Provide monthly photo updates on growth and development and record major milestone achievements.

Doctor/Pharmacist/Butt Wiper

Administer various drugs for teething, colds, sinus infections, etc. Aspirate nose when stuffed up, wipe butt when poopy, pump legs up and down when gassy.

Salon and Spa Technician

Administer bubble bath, maintain proper water temperature, towel dry all parts, apply lotion, brush hair. Give massage treatments, routine manicures and pedicures.

Personal Chef

Prepare all meals (Nursing moms are in charge of milk, of course). Maintain supply. Provide a variety of fruits, grains, vegetables, and desserts. Keep bottles clean and sanitized. Wash bowls, spoons and sippy cups after every use. Provide a steady supply of teething biscuits.
Or taking one from HBO... we're planning to have t-shirts made that simply read...

Ada's Entourage

Moral of the story: As parents, you must learn to wear many hats and juggle many positions. Unfortunately, these skills aren't widely recognized by employers if you need to pad your resume.

October

First Camping Trip

Ada's first camping trip was gloriously uneventful. We didn't see any bears or raccoons. There weren't any mosquitoes since it was on the chilly side—fifty to sixty degrees I'd say. And we didn't spend the night and actually "camp" in tents as we normally would since the overnight temperatures were in the mid-thirties. That just wasn't my idea of fun.

Instead, Rick chauffeured Ada and I up to Marengo Ridge for the day. We left early in order to arrive for breakfast. At first we arrived at the wrong camp area but were quickly redirected to the group site. After some trouble with the combination to the lock on the gate that delayed us from entering the group camp area, we were met at the parking lot by Grandpa Rich, Grandma Ba, Uncle Shawn and various family friends. They anticipated having to help us carry all of our "camping gear" which was really just Ada's diaper bag, blankets, extra clothes, food, and toys. We didn't even take camping chairs with us. And it was so nice just to show up and be taken care of. With someone holding the baby and everyone else holding most of her stuff, I carried my knitting bag and camera down to the campsite.

When we arrived at the site, we were greeted as if we had just woken up and crawled out from our tent. Hot cinnamon rolls from the Dutch oven were fresh off the campfire. We have the world's greatest camping chef who camps with our group. Tom is the master of all things camping, and has a knack for dutch ovens. You name it, he can make it. Birthday cake, pineapple upside down cake, biscuits, rolls, etc., and all of it delicious. After inhaling the cinnamon roll, we got settled on a blanket in the sun with Ada and her toys sprawled around us. Then we placed our omelet order. Somehow I got to be at the top of the list and was first to enjoy my ham and American cheese omelet hot off the propane stove. Then I shared an order of biscuits and gravy with Rick, had some bacon on the side, and decided life was good.

Ada had a jar of green beans and rice and some prunes. Boy did she ever get the short end of that deal.

After breakfast, Ada took a nap, woke up, got passed around from person to person for a million cuddles, and then took another nap. She did well sleeping in on air mattress in Grandma and Grandpa's tent. When she awoke from her second nap of the day, she momentarily caused a bit of alarm in the campsite when she grabbed a hold of the rain fly covering the tent and started shaking it vigorously, similar to what we all imagine it would look like if a raccoon got into your tent and started rustling around. Someone quickly called out, "Ada's up!" and everyone went back to the calm state of relaxation they were enjoying. I of course, rolled over from my nap and got up to feed her. Lucky me.

Sometime during the day, Great Aunt Connie arrived with brownies—triple chocolate brownies to be exact—and life got really good. I got some knitting projects completed, Ada got a ton of attention, Rick got to play poker and read. All in all, a great day. We decided to stick around for dinner—roast beef sandwiches—and then took off for the drive home. A highlight of the camping trip was that we only had to drive an hour and a half to get there and then the same on the return. And since Ada really doesn't sleep in the car much, that was a real bonus.

Now I just had about six loads of laundry to do to get the smoke out of everything we took with us.

Moral of the story: Camping is a lot of fun when you don't have to do anything but show up with the baby and her stuff and can let someone else take care of the rest. Oh, and good weather helps.

If You Squint, You Can See It

The eagle has landed...

If you blink, you'll miss it...

Some things are worth the wait...

It's about friggin' time it showed itself...

Yes.

It has arrived.

Dun dun dunnnnnnnnnn... (Imagine some really cheesy music here.)

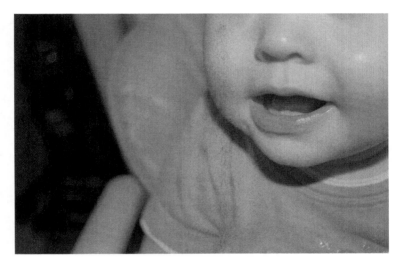

"What?" you ask.

HER TOOTH, SILLY!

Can't you see it in the photo clear as day?

No? You can't see it? Well. Obviously you are blind! Squint a little harder.

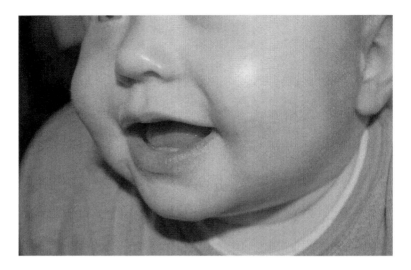

Okay, so you can't see it because NEWSFLASH a baby's tooth isn't easy to photograph (without an x-ray machine that is) AND they don't come shooting up all at once like you see in the movies. Gesh!

But it's here. Her lower right front tooth has finally—after about six months of pissing her off to no end and driving us all nuts—decided to show up. Thank goodness.

Moral of the story: If you ever have to photograph a baby's tooth, make sure you have two people, flip her upside down, tickler her while hopping on one foot and you might, just maybe, still end up with a whole lot of nothing.

My First Face-Plant

Yep. She's finally done it. Someone should have started an office pool for when it would happen but ... too late now. Ada had her first face-plant today. She went to the park with Nanny Ashley and decided to fall face first into the wood chips on the playground. She was sitting so sweet and innocent on the end of the toddler slide and whoop, waaaaaaahhhhhhhhhh! Down she went. The good thing was her spirits were still up and her cuts were minor... and pink (the color of scratches and cuts) really was a good color on her.

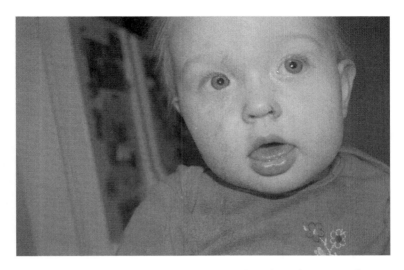

Moral of the story: Babies fall. That's what they do. We pick 'em up, dust 'em off, pretend nothing happened and move on. And just be thankful that even if they are all scraped up, they are still cuter than most adults (and some puppies).

Up, Up & Away!

This past weekend was Ada's first plane ride since being out of the womb. I was nervous all week and not really looking forward to traveling with an infant since I didn't enjoy the whole process of flying all that much to begin with. Surprisingly, it wasn't that bad. It wasn't good, but it wasn't so bad that I was never doing it again, bad.

Unlike our long trip to Germany via Ireland with a sprint through the airport to catch a connecting flight in June while I was three-months pregnant and very unhappy about flying, this trip was about a three hour flight from Chicago to Boston. Not bad.

We took off twenty minutes early (shocking, I know!) and were able to pack light as Rick's sister was able to borrow a crib, car seat, toys, blankets, etc. so that we didn't need to pack much. I took Ada in her Ergo carrier and that was easy. We also left on a Saturday night with a six fifty-five departure. NOBODY flies on Saturday nights this time of year so there were no lines.

Okay, maybe I waited behind Rick in line at the security check but then I decided he had too much crap (keys, money, wallet, watch, shoes, belt, etc.) and I'd be better off in the other line. I took off my shoes, put my purse in the x-ray bin and walked through with Ada attached to me. So easy. Then we had to hike to our gate since it was on the other end of the state it seemed, but we got there in time to eat the dinner we brought with us, change her into footie pajamas for the trip, and change her diaper one last time.

The flight was uneventful, thankfully. We arrived. Heather and Matt were there to pick us up and all was well until they lost the car in the parking garage. Twenty minutes later, after a long walk up and down aisle after aisle, Matt finally realized we were one floor above the car, but in the right section. We loaded up the stuff, Ada passed out almost instantly, and we started the hour and a half journey to the farm, ending in Brooklyn, Connecticut. We had a minor blip with the toll booth exit and detoured for a minute but finally arrived and nestled into our beds right around midnight.

Rise and Shine! Baby woke up early and it didn't matter if we didn't get much sleep because it was time to go see the horses and play on the farm. In the two days we were there, we got way more than just quality time with Aunt Heather and Uncle Matt. We saw horses, cows, baby cows—that scared Ada when they mooed—hay being baled, really big draft horses, the pet cemetery on the farm, the local ice cream shop—yum, hot waffle cones fresh off the iron—and Matt's friend Sam's one-hundred-and-one-year-old grandma who was out picking weeds! I learned that I needed a whole new vocabulary and my own Carhart overalls in order to really fit in. And a highlight of the trip was the resident deer in the front yard. A momma and two babies came to visit each day for the freshly fallen nuts from the trees. All good things.

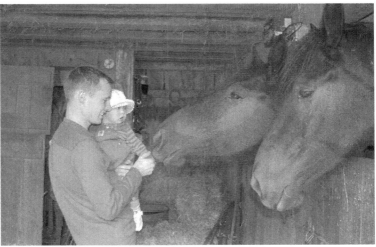

Then the trip home. Well, let's just say it was tough. We got up at three in the morning our time and got home about eleven. That made for a long day with a fussy little miss. It was a great time to drive in Boston but a crappy time to get a baby to nap and not want to play and be entertained on the plane.

Highlight: We saw John Kerry at the airport—and I almost ran into him as he came out of the book store. Very cool. He was flying to Milwaukee.

Oh, and Heather and Matt were awesome. They were doing great. Their home was adorable and enormous compared to our little box in the city. They had four bedrooms, two bathrooms and a basement after all. And the farm was soooo quiet. Nothing like the city. You stood on the front porch and heard nothing but your heart beat and the red squirrels in the leaves ten feet in front of you. Crazy how quiet it was. You didn't really have to look both ways before crossing the street because you could hear any car coming for at least a hundred yards, or two hundred if it was Matt's diesel truck.

I decided it needed to be an annual or almost-annual retreat and that next time we would stay longer, eat more yummy food, and keep Ada to a stricter schedule as she did break down due to the lack of structure.

Moral of the story: Traveling with little ones is manageable assuming they aren't sick, you aren't sick, you travel light, and you don't have a bunch of crab apples on your plane who are all ticked off that your kid won't shut up. Just ignore them.

I Wish I Could Still Fit in the Sink

I didn't think I had anything exciting to report, but then I checked the camera for recent photos of Ada.

Here's what I found...

Amanda H. Young

I wish I could still have someone bathe me in the sink.

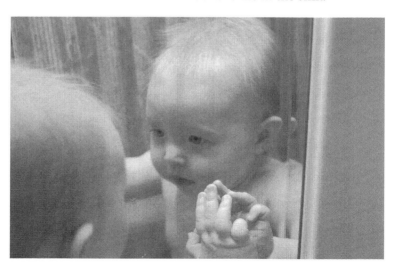

152

Remember when life was this easy? Ada loves the mirror.

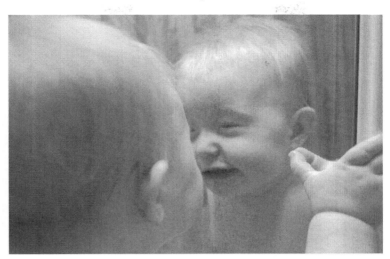

And she can entertain herself for hours.

Other than that, not much else to report on the Ada scene. Her tooth is still coming in. She's still trying to crawl. She's getting better at stealing toys back from Eva on their playdates. And she's still not on a napping schedule. But she's sleeping through the night—fourteen hours straight is still the record. And she's still having whiny moments where she gets so frustrated from not being able to crawl yet that she just screams. I think we all have those moments in life.

Moral of the story: Just go look in a mirror and smile. Someone will smile right back at you. Then you can make faces at them, and they'll make faces back too.

More Teeth!

Finally, the onslaught begins. Ada has her two front teeth popping through now too! And we've found a new use for her "Soothie", which is another brand of pacifier or "Nuk". She uses it at a teething toy since it is hard plastic that she can get into the hard to reach places in her mouth and it doesn't hurt as much as chomping on her fingers.

If you squint, you might be able to see the three teeth here. One bottom, two top. Pretty exciting!

Moral of the story: Almost everything you own will become a teething toy at some point.

I'm a Little Toucan, Short & Feathery

Rick and I know Ada is going to hate us for this when she gets older, but who could resist? She's just so cute!

And the best part?

The costume is from a school fundraiser garage sale in our home town and was purchased by Grandma Ba.
The leggings are from Aunt Anne and will last all winter long.
The socks and the long-sleeve red Onesie are hand-me-downs.

The next best part?

She fell asleep five blocks from the party after not having taken a nap all day. Of course, we then had to wake her up for the party. And she slept the whole way home—all twenty-five minutes.

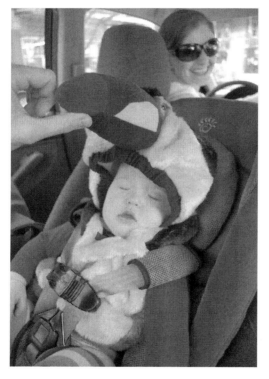

Cost of looking adorable on Halloween? Nada.

Thanks to all who help Ada always look cute.

Moral of the story: Don't spend a ton on kids' Halloween costumes. Kids are so cute to begin with that it doesn't take much to exploit that fact and make a good costume out of a sheet and some pipe cleaners.

The Formula Formula

Ada's ten-months old and we're ready for a little formula. So how does that work?

Well, we don't know.

Rick and I have been talking about introducing a bit of baby formula for weeks now as my milk supply is okay but not bountiful, and we'd like it if I was less tethered to the baby, less stressed about having enough milk supply and just as a fall-back plan in case we need it. I have about nine ounces in the freezer, but that's not a whole lot when she's eating more than that each day. I'm still nursing her four times a day when I'm home, two times a day if I work. And I still pump each night before bed and mid-day at work assuming we don't have a lot of milk in the fridge and I'm not on a deadline. But I can make it eight hours without nursing now, if need be, and it is not the end of the world.

So yesterday, we tried a little formula in a bottle. Oh boy.

She hated it!

She had a look as if to say, "Wow, what a fun toy you've given me. A bottle with sticky stuff that I can drip all over myself." She tasted it. Then made a funny face and proceeded to play with the bottle and make a mess. We tried a generic soy-based formula to begin with as I'm told it is easier to digest, but I think we're going to have to try something else. We'll give this formula another chance or two since it is only good now for a month and we have a whole container of it, but I'm not confident that she's going to go for it. At least we have less than two months before we can make the switch to whole cow's milk. Hopefully that goes better than this little experiment.

Moral of the story: As a parent, you'll find that you often have no clue what you're doing. That's okay. Just keep researching, trying new things, and asking moms who have gone before you. We can't all be clueless.

Where Have All of the Naps Gone?

Our little rock star napper has turned into a napless little fuss pot. Ada used to take two naps a day, sometimes even three. But lately, she was on to our little plan to sing her to sleep and rock away the fun. She was putting up such a fight that she spent more time trying not to go to sleep than actually sleeping. And then she did silly things like fall asleep on the way to a party, but not until we were five blocks away. She didn't normally even sleep in the car, unless of course it was a really short trip that we didn't want her to sleep during. Then, she was out.

Today was the ultimate battle of teething and refusing to nap. As eleven rolled around, I assumed she was hungry as she hadn't eaten since seven in the morning and, what did she do? She fell asleep while nursing. So typical. And even more frustrating, we had a lunch date at noon that we had to cancel so she could get her beauty rest. Such was the life of having a baby. It was still worth it.

I must say, I would rather she were a mess during the day and off her schedule then instead of during the night. We were still very blessed to have a daughter who slept eleven or twelve hours a night. For that I was very thankful.

Moral of the story: Don't get lulled into a false sense of security when your child adheres to a schedule for awhile. Enjoy it, but know that it isn't likely to last and be thankful for what naps and sleep you do get.

We're Mobile!

AHHH!!!!!!!!

Ada just learned to crawl. Do they make martini IVs for moms?

Moral of the story: Milestones can be emotional. Try to stay calm.

November

The time came for us to try giving Ada formula again this weekend. Unfortunately, we got into a situation where I went to a wedding and had a good time that included a few chocolate martinis—for which I needed to pump-n-dump as they say—and our milk supply dropped to an all-time low. It didn't help that upon returning from the wedding reception and a night out on the town until two in the morning like the crazy mom that I am—in a short sassy black dress mind you—I woke up around five to begin a twelve hour bout with the flu and some quality time praising the porcelain gods. Rick got a head start on the flu during the reception dinner and had to call it an early night. Our house was a sad state Saturday morning and our only saving grace was that my mom had come to stay with us to babysit Ada during the wedding. My poor mom had to listen to Rick and I both get sick, while dealing with a crabby Ada, and exposing herself to all of our cooties. Thankfully she didn't get the full-blown version of the bug we got. It was awful.

So we took everyone's advice and mixed Ada's formula 50/50 with breast milk and it worked like a charm. She guzzled it down the first time. Then this afternoon we tried again and she drank the concoction just fine. Then she had dinner and while lounging on the couch, she started round two of the flu—if you know what we mean. We've become experts in running the couch cushions through the laundry machine at this point.

Moral of the story: 50/50 is the way to go when switching to formula but when buying a couch, make sure the cushions are 100% washable... pretty much the same rule goes for everything you buy if you ever plan to have kids.

Mom Group Halloween

The Mom Network at the hospital has a Halloween party every year and a bunch of Ada's friends were there. Of course, we tried to take a photo of all of the kids in their adorable costumes. Ada's the blue toucan. Here's what happened...

Total chaos.

Moral of the story: I don't know how Anne Geddes does it (maybe while they are sleeping?) but photographing multiple kids at once isn't easy. Be sure to get it all out of your system before they go mobile.

Who Needs a Pack 'n Play?

So brilliant me thought I was so smart to put Ada in a laundry basket to contain her in the kitchen while I checked my email. It was like a mini Pack 'n Play, yet light and easy to move and maneuver. She was happy and all was well, until she decided to tip it over and fell face first onto the hard kitchen tile. Whoops! Not such a great idea after all. Not such a smarty mommy either.

Moral of the story: Sometimes what might seem like a good plan just isn't. Luckily babies get bumps and bruises and take it in stride. Just try to minimize the damage.

When Panic Strikes

Three times this last week I've had to calm my mom instinct and repress the urge to immediately panic. The first was when Ada was holding on to the side of the bath tub and chewing on the porcelain when she somehow bonked her teeth on the tub edge. She started screaming and upon further evaluation, I noticed she was bleeding a little from her two front teeth. Instant almost-panic. I took a deep breath, checked her teeth again, wiped away the blood, and then took another deep breath. She was fine. I shook it off. No biggie. Crisis averted.

Then I worried that Ada had broken something when she decided to hurl herself off our bed. I was standing right there, between the bed and the closet. I turned for part of a second and she was able to launch herself off the edge of the bed, roll onto the floor and land on top of Rick's shoe with her cheekbone. After a minute of extreme screaming and a few tears, she settled down enough to reveal a red mark on her cheek that later turned into a bruise. Another crisis averted.

And finally, when I went in to get her out of bed on Thursday, she was covered with vomit. Not having had her really throw up ever before, I wasn't sure what to do with her. I immediately assumed it was a food allergy and stuck her in the shower with Rick to get cleaned up. A few hours later, our nanny called to say Ada had thrown up all over the couch and wasn't feeling well. Then she remembered one of the kids on Ada's playdate had been sick. That led Rick home to stay with Ada for the day and me to make her an appointment with the doctor. It was just a case of the flu. She'll be fine. We just had to keep her hydrated.

Moral of the story: Do all you can to prevent your child from getting injured or sick, and remember not to panic if something should happen. It's probably not as bad as you think. Stay calm.

Kitten Mittens

Winter is officially here. We saw a few snowflakes today and decided it was time to pull out Ada's winter coat. It looked a little big but we thought we'd try it on her anyway. So here it is.

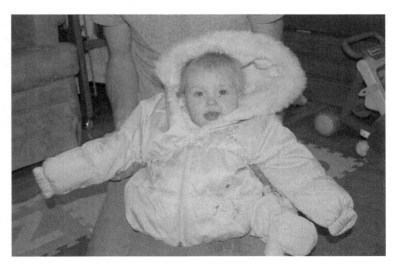

Where's Ada? Okay, so maybe she's not ready for a twenty-four-month coat quite yet. We tried. Maybe next year. Until we grab a proper coat, we'll be using the kitten mittens, matching kitten hat, and many layers of hooded sweatshirts and coats. And we'll be coat shopping tomorrow.

Moral of the story: It's tough to gauge how big a growing baby will be next season, but even tougher for a generous mother-in-law to pass up a sale. Always be thankful for that.

Successful Formula!

It worked. Believe it or not—I still have trouble believing it—it worked. Ada is now drinking 100% formula. She graduated from the half and half mix to all formula and it rocks. I nurse her whenever I feel like it. She drinks formula whenever I think she didn't get enough breast milk. She's happy. I'm happy. Life is beautiful.

I don't have to pump anymore—which by the way is AWESOME! It is so much easier to travel with her and I think I'm getting more sleep now that I'm not up twenty minutes extra each night pumping. I feel like I'm washing fewer bottles but really it's probably more bottles and less pump stuff. What a relief. And, driving with her is easier too as I can easily whip up a bottle whenever we need it. Very nice. No complaints here. I made it over ten months strictly nursing and it was a huge sacrifice but worth it. And now I feel great with a little bit of both. She'll be on whole cow's milk soon enough.

Too bad she's back to teething again. Poor little thing. She has four teeth and these past few days have been awful with her drooling and screaming and not napping and waking up during the night. And Tylenol isn't even helping. Ug. But, like all things thus far, we'll get through it.

Oh, and I'm also so excited since now that Ada is drinking formula, we can send her to grandma's house for the weekend and not have to worry about if she has enough milk. Perfect for the holidays coming up since we have a few parties to attend and really just don't want to dole out a million dollars for babysitters.

Moral of the story: Weaning your child isn't the worst thing on earth as some people might suggest. It's actually quite freeing, and helps you see how much you've dedicated to your child if you did nurse them. Kinda rewarding.

Give Me a P!

So today, in typical Ada fashion, I was changing her diaper and she was squirming around like a normal eleven-month old. She started out on the changing table but got too wiggly so I decided the floor would be safer. In her room we have an alphabet mat made of foam where all the letters of the alphabet link together in interlocking pieces—it was great as a shock absorber when she fell and looked cool too.

As I went to set her down on the mat, she of course wanted to stand up—it was tough to get her little knees to bend when all she wanted to do was stand up. ALL of the time. So she was naked, standing up. There was a poopy diaper on the changing table and I was trying to grab the wipes, put the cloth diaper in the diaper cover while holding her up and what did she do? She peed all over the letter P, while standing, mind you. So now I had a poopy diaper, a pee-covered P and surrounding tiles, and a pee-covered Ada who now, of course, wanted to sit down and started crawling all over so she could spread the wealth of pee to the rest of the letters. Luckily, she was only able to grab her elephant rattle before I was able to wrap her in a cloth diaper haphazardly and briskly walk down the hall to the bathroom hoping pee wasn't dripping all through the house as I whisked her off to the sink.

I gave her a quick rinse while fighting to keep her from

scorching herself as she found it really fun to play with the faucet knobs. Once she was "clean" which was a relative term and only a temporary state at this age, I toweled her off, again attempted the diaper dance and was able to successfully finagle her into her diaper. I quickly returned her to the far end of her play mat and then removed the peed on P and the elephant rattle and the poopy diaper and the wet diaper from her room. Who knew multitasking was such a prerequisite for being a parent? Whew.

Moral of the story: Don't put a P on the floor. You're just asking for it to be peed on simply for the irony of it all.

The New Drawer

Awhile back, several months ago now, Grandma DD (my mom) came to visit. She often comes to take care of Ada and, among other things, clean the stove and the refrigerator and all the fun stuff like that we no longer care, or have time, to do anymore. So DD was here cleaning and tried to open the top drawer under our kitchen counter. She couldn't open it so what did she do? She pulled with all of her might until it opened, darn it. When it did, she was in for a surprise. It wasn't really a drawer at all. She had pulled off the face plate to what would be a drawer in any normal home, but the developers who remodeled our building failed to install a drawer in the top slot of the cabinet. It's the same in all of the kitchens in our building because they were stock cabinets meant for a bathroom and therefore should have a sink basin that dips into the space a drawer would slide into, thereby making a top drawer unnecessary. In our case, they just covered the cabinet with a granite slab, didn't go to the trouble of installing the missing drawer and said, "Whatever, no one will notice."

No one, except my mom.

See my mom is a Realtor. She snoops around houses for a living. And she's a practical woman too. You can imagine her surprise to find a "fake" drawer in my kitchen. And you can imagine my surprise upon returning home to find Ada napping and happy and my mom holding on to the face of my cabinet drawer wondering what just happened. Then for the followup reaction, "Rick can totally go to Home Depot and get a drawer for this and you'll have more storage space. You can't just leave it fake. That's silly."

Two weeks of waiting for the special order drawer, $30, and five hours of fiddling with the darn cabinet later, we had a functioning drawer. Which was great and we had a home for our oven mitts and a few trivets. Yippee! I was sure our resale value went up at least $5 for that effort, right?

The drawer is great, except for a teeny, tiny, itsy, bitsy problem. Rick had to install a new drawer slide and the new one was way better than all of the other drawer slides because it had two rollers on the sides instead of one roller in the middle on the bottom of the drawer. It was metal with plastic wheels whereas the rest of the drawers were wood on wood slides with a plastic do-hicky and no wheels. Think lots of friction. The new one slides really nice and fast now and all of the other drawers are jealous. That wasn't the problem. The problem was that Ada wanted to pull up on all of the drawers so she could stand up. And when she climbed from the lower drawers that didn't move so easily to the top drawer that did, she wiped out. She grabbed the handle and Whoop! down she went. An accident just waiting to happen.

Here's Ada just prior to wipe out.

Moral of the story: You can't plan for everything. Even good intentions for increased resale value can go bad in the tear-filled eyes of a child. She still loves you DD.

The Grocery Shopping Challenge

Who knew it was so hard to do something as simple as grocery shop when you had a baby? Finding time to shop was part of the issue. Having the energy to make a list, check the cupboard, run around the store, lug the groceries back into the house, and put them away—that was a whole different story. There was a reason grocery delivery services existed. There was a need for grocery delivery when you were a mom.

Today, I was sitting at work, with eight programs open on my computer and in the middle of five different things when I noticed, "Shoot" (my G rated version), "It's already four thirty. I gotta get to the store." I typically left work at four forty-five, raced to the car, and road raged home in a hurry—counteracting my rage by driving through the park since it was more calming, scenic, and if I'm being honest, faster. Then I was usually five minutes late because I would have to circle for parking once, unless I got really lucky and found a spot out front.

As I was finishing things up on my computer, I grabbed my cell phone to call the nanny and tell her I would be ten minutes late. I quickly closed out of everything I was working on, clicked send on one last email, told the guys that I would update them on a potential lead once I knew more and I left. I got outside, briskly walked—trotted actually—to the car, got in and realized it was winter. I would have to wait to heat up the car. I never waited to heat up the car and I knew it wasn't good on the engine so I was trying to train myself early this season to be good to my little Honda because she was good to me. So I tried to wait one minute for the clock to turn to 4:42 from 4:41 and... I couldn't do it. I made it forty seconds and put it in drive.

Vroom, vroom, beep, beep. Seriously? Just turn left already. Hurry up people! Learn how to drive in the city. Don't make me miss this light you turtle! Gas is on the right! Let's go, let's go, let's go.

Six blocks later, I pulled into the grocery store. "Oops! (G rated version) I forgot my reusable shopping bags. Oh well. There goes the environment." It's four fifty. I parked, hustled into the store. Grabbed a basket and called Colette to see if she needed anything last minute. Her list was too long for me to get in one quick trip so she declined my offer, but I tried. Ta ta.

Here I go. First on the list, formula. Oh, look! Baby food is on sale. Let's get a few jars, or twenty. Whatever. Wow. This basket is heavy. Hmmm... next on the list. Oh, wait. I have to get dinner for tonight. A roasted chicken and some bread sounds good. I'll grab a cart while I'm by the front door. My arm hurts from all these baby food jars. Geesh. Got a cart with a crummy wheel/vibrating mis-alignment thing going on. Nice. Eeert, eert. I whipped through the produce aisle. Roasted chickens are $9.99? That can't be right. Oh, that's the turkey breast. I need the chicken. Got it. Eeert, eert, chitty chitty bang

bang. Fresh baked bread. Italian or French? Italian. Nice. Hot out of the oven. Love it. Chitty chitty. What's next? Chocolate for work so I can feed my cravings. Ziplock bags—the big ones, and pecans for the divinity I'm going to attempt tonight. Okay. Chocolate, might be near the nuts. Let's see. Eeeert, chugga chugga, Snickers aren't on sale but Kit-Kats are. Should I really be doing this? Ah, what the heck. It's the holidays and I need something sweet darn it (again G rated). Okay, so the nuts in the chocolate aisle don't include pecans. Let's try the baking aisle. Yep. There we go. Chortle chortle. I attempted to "spin" the cart around. Ziplock. Two aisles over. Yeah, on sale. Freezer or no freezer? I don't want the vacuum seal. Freezer sounds great. Now to check out. Wow those lines are longgggggggg. What's up with checkout line number two....looks empty. "Are you open?"

"Yeah, I just opened."

"Nice. This is my lucky day." Yada yada.

I got behind a slow couple leaving the store, dur dur dur, dur dur dur. Finally, I got into the parking lot.

I attempted to ride the cart out to my car but it was vibrating so violently that I feared for my life. I went back to trotting behind it in my heeled boots, clop clopping along. Where did I park? I think I'm one row over. Oh, there it is. I loaded the bags into the trunk. Great. The chicken bag handle broke already. That will be fun getting into the house.

I pushed the cart into the cart corral, yea ha! I went back to the car and vroom vroom home. More road rage, impatience, get out of my way.

Okay, there's my street. Slow guy in front of me. Don't take my spot, don't take my spot. What? No spots near the house. Oh wait, no! Someone just pulled into a prime spot right in front of our house! Urg! Five twenty-five. I'm late. I have groceries to carry inside! Have you no heart? Do you even live on this street? Grrrrr... Around the block, cut through the alley, try again. Is this really as close as I can get? I'm half a block away. Whatever. It's five twenty-eight. I'm so late. I told the nanny ten minutes and it's almost thirty now. Go go go.

I parked quickly, popped the trunk, grabbed all six grocery bags and the broken bag holding the chicken. I checked that the car was locked and click, clacketey clacked quickly down the street.

I was just over half way home and I noticed the clacking start to slow.

These bags are heavy. Must make it home. You can do it! What? Are you flippin' kidding me (super G rated)? You're going to leave now? Why not thirty seconds ago when I was looking for a spot right in front of the door. Urg. No time. Get inside!

Finally, I got to the front door.

Do I buzz or find my key?

I set everything down, found the key, unlocked the first vestibule door and held it open with my hip and my foot. I grabbed all of the bags and the broken chicken bag. I got inside, climbed the four steps, and opened the second vestibule door. Then I got to the front door. I tried the lock, set it all down again, got out the key, and unlocked the door. Finally I was home.

"Sorry I'm late. Of course I parked down the street and when I got ten steps from the front door I noticed a Jeep out front pulling out of the spot directly in front of the door. How aggravating. Have a good night. See you in the morning."

"Hey there Ada. Want to help mommy take the groceries to the kitchen? What? You can't walk yet? Bummer. Soon enough." I grabbed all of the handles and the chicken bag and shuffled back into the kitchen with Ada in tow.

And that folks, was what it took to buy a few items from the store. Forty-five minutes, $56 dollars, two missed parking opportunities, two bouts of road rage, getting stuck behind no less than eight slow people, and an aching arm later, I had a few items to attempt to make a candy my Grandma Nana made for us every holiday when we were younger that we hadn't had since she passed. All that work and who knew if it would even turn out.

Moral of the story: This Thanksgiving, I give thanks for Peapod (when I have a $100 order to make it worthwhile to pay for delivery), family, attempting to cook, having the access to readily available food at grocery stores, and the freedom to cook as poorly as I do without being jailed for it. I'm hopeful that next year I'll be able to give thanks for patience as I've put that on my Christmas list this year. If you see Santa, let him know.

December

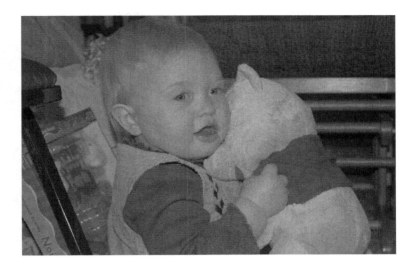

Pinned In

Today, Ada and I ventured out in the snow to see her doctoress. Ada had a cold for about a week and a half with a hefty cough that just wouldn't leave. With the holidays behind us and all of our tricks making little difference to hurry this cold on its way, it was time to visit the doctoress and make sure this cootie was shown the door.

We set aside an hour to get ready but could have easily used two. I left ample time, or so I thought, to clean the snow off the car as we accumulated about two inches overnight. Unfortunately, as I was putting Ada's socks and shoes on her squirmy little feet, a waft of something not-so-pleasant hit me and we were delayed a few minutes as I re-changed her diaper that was a whole five-minutes old, and disposed of the toxic waste in the back dumpster. I took about twenty seconds to debate wearing tennis shoes or golashes and chose the golashes. After all, why bother trying to be fashionable when taking a sick kid to the doctoress when you didn't have time to put makeup on, it snowed recently and was sure to be slushy, and you weren't going to see anyone you knew?

I got Ada ready and realized that she needed a hat, and I needed to grab the diaper bag. Oh, and I needed my phone. Ooooh, and I should grab some food and make her a bottle before we left. Tick, tock. Tick tock. Thank goodness I padded my schedule with some extra time for all this last minute stuff.

We loaded up, or I should say, I grabbed Ada, the diaper bag, the shoulder bag serving as my purse these days, my hat, gloves, a scarf, my jacket, double checked I had keys, hoisted the baby onto my hip and we were out the front door, first and second vestibule doors and into the fresh, cold, winter air. The car was right out front and I located my keys, unlocked the door and heaved Ada inside as I stepped into the puddle next to the curb. Thank goodness I was wearing my golashes! I was now standing in six inches of brown, cold, slush, but my feet were dry. I locked Ada down into her car seat and grabbed my gloves when they got hooked on my sunglasses and, of course, I flung the glasses into the brown slush below. At least they were plastic and would wash easily. Tragedy narrowly avoided.

Ada cried as I danced around the car ridding it of snow. I got in. She started to really cry. I got out. I gave her a bottle of milk. I got back in and pulled out. Our appointment was at eleven forty-five and it was eleven thirty-five. It was a ten minute drive so we were cutting it close. We got five blocks away and she started screaming. She dropped the bottle onto the seat beside her. I got to a red stop light, got out, gave her the bottle and propped it up better this time. I got in. We made it another five blocks and she dropped it again but this time she wasn't hysterical. Five more blocks and we arrived at our destination. We did the whole doctoress visit. Ada got a flu shot. The doctoress said she was fine, but she might have an infection and we could try Amoxicillin in a few days if it didn't clear up on its own. I scheduled my flu shot for later in the week, and Ada's one-year vaccine appointment and we were off. We bundled back up, I gathered all of our stuff and "bye bye", we headed out to the car.

Now, on to our errand of the day. We were stopping by The Right Start to pick up a second car seat so that we could swap it between grandparent's cars and carry my niece if ever we needed to. It was on sale and the sale ended today, of course. So we drove up to the store and there was prime parking available, but it was squished in between two cars and it was a tight fit. So what. I was going to squeeze into it and show that green jeep who was boss. I mean really. Who parks like that? So we squeezed in. We shimmied out on the driver's side as I have left more room for me to get out than for them to get in on the right side. Serves them right.

Once in the store, we learned that they only had the pink one in stock. Was that okay? "Sure. That's what we wanted in the first place but it wasn't in stock." I called Rick to confirm and all was well. (You may remember a bit of drama we had about not being able to get the pink one. Well, we now have a pink one.)

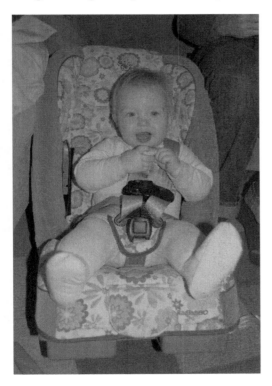

After waiting in line—this place was really busy for two on a Monday—the nice saleswoman carried it to my car. The green Jeep had moved so it was easy to get it past the car and into the trunk. She returned to the store and left me to put Ada into her car seat. With the Jeep gone, it was easier for me to load Ada into the car on the passenger side, too. I followed her into the back seat and shut the door to keep out the cold. As I was strapping Ada in, a grey mini van pulled next to us. The driver realized she was too close and couldn't get out, but like me, she felt this was too good of a spot to pass up. So she realigned the van a few inches and slipped out of the van and into the store. Now that Ada was secured, it was my turn to slip out. But I couldn't. It was too tight.

Served me right. Karma always came back to bite you in the butt. And boy did it ever bite me. Sitting in the back seat with my golashes on, I threw my leg over Ada in the car seat, and shimmied to the driver's side of the back seat so that I could open the driver's side door. I eventually got behind the wheel, all while avoiding crushing Ada's little body in her car seat as she looked at me thinking, "What the hell are you doing, Mom?"

As I was doing this shimmy thing in the back seat, I was also on the phone with Rick discussing the purchase, the doctoress visit and the irony of the green Jeep turning into the grey van and how I was now stuck. I was straddling Ada and the car seat while on the phone when, "Oh shit. Ow. OW. OWWW. That hurts. Rick hold on."
"Are you okay Amanda?" he asked as I was holding the phone at arms length as I stretched out a cramp under my floating rib. "Yeah, I'm fine. Sorry about that. I got a cramp while suspended over Ada. Karma always gets even." We wrapped up our conversation and Ada and I headed home.

Of course, we got an okay parking spot. Nothing fabulous but at least it was on our street. I figured it was residual karma backlash and hoped that doing a few good deeds early in the day tomorrow would set things back to the good side of things.

Moral of the story: If it's crummy outside, wear your golashes. If a space is too tight, no matter how close it is to the door, let it go. You could probably use the exercise and it's better than a cramp under your rib and a game of Twister to get back into the car.

Everything but the Kitchen Sink

Packing for the holidays was never all that easy, but it was even harder when you had a munchkin in tow. Each time we packed for a weekend or an overnight with Ada, we always ended up taking too much of everything, not enough of the things we needed, and forgot the really important stuff—like a poop-filled diaper on the middle of the nursery floor when we expected to be gone for several days. (Huge thanks go to our neighbor Kelly for using our spare keys to eliminate that threat as we remembered it an hour away from home.)

This time was no different. We each had a bag of clothes. Ada had a bag of clothes, a bag of blankets (we have radiators and it was always much warmer here than anywhere else hence all of the blankets), a bag of diapers and wipes, a diaper bag, and probably another bag I'm forgetting. Oh, and her carrier just in case. Then we had all the stuff we had to take with us, things to entertain us in the car, things to eat, things we made for other people to eat. You get the point. Way too much stuff for a three-day trip.

So it really wasn't surprising when I said that the nanny called me at work at ten asking where all of Ada's formula was. Uh... "It is all in the trunk. I packed it. All of it." Yep. I told you I forgot to mention another bag. Ada had a food bag and a carry-on food bag that didn't go in the trunk. Unfortunately, I had packed it all in the trunk before going to work so I wouldn't have to pack with her alone in the house or alone in the car or in the carrier on my back as I schlepped all of the crap out to the car. "I'll be right home." But the nanny offered to hold Ada off and give her water and baby food until I got home right after lunch to feed her milk. I had a few things to get done at work and, the guilty mom that I was, I left at noon instead of one thirty so that my baby wouldn't starve to death or be deprived her milk fix for the morning. Bad mommy.

Upon returning home to find Ada crawling around in an obnoxious outfit while barefoot, I was quickly reminded (by the nanny) that I had indeed packed all of her "cool" stuff— Including her cool shoes, clothes, hats, gloves, bibs... all of it— forcing her to look like a complete dork that morning. She'll get me back someday. I'm pretty sure of it.

And to make things even more interesting, since we had Ada's car seat already installed in our car, we got to play chauffeur to my family for the three hours to our relatives' house for Thanksgiving in our four-door Honda Civic. Normally that would be fine but we got to do it with a baby, all of the baby's stuff, all of our clothes for an overnight at my cousin's house with blankets for us and Ada, all of the food my dad was going to prepare, a Pack 'n Play for Ada, and four adults in the car—three being men 5'9" and above. Lovely.

Moral of the story: Be sure to give a responsible neighbor your house keys, just in case. And try to pack light. There is only so much room in the trunk of a Honda Civic.

Rockin' It Retro

It's winter and it's cold. I mentioned how Ada needed a winter coat that fit her. The first one we had was too big. My mom went out and got her a coat at Target that was cute and we were using it. At the same time, my mother-in-law went into her basement and found something a little more retro—as in thirty-years retro. She still had Rick's winter coat from when he was a baby, and his brother wore it, and his sister wore it, and now Ada was wearing it. It fit great, looked cute and was free. It was in great shape too so we would be sure to pass it on to the next baby in the family. Who knows what else will turn up from Grandma Ba's basement. We'll just have to wait and see.

How's that for recycling?

Moral of the story: Vintage fashion can be cool, especially when it is something your dad wore when he was little.

The Blank Snow Globe

This past weekend we learned a little factoid about the consequences of naming our daughter something unique and more unusual. Even though she's named after great great grandmothers on both sides of our family, Ada isn't a very common name nowadays.

While at my parents' house, I was perusing a shelf of trinkets and noticed that my dad had purchased mini snow globes with all of our names on them. There was Bob, Diane, Rick, Amanda, Rob, Anna and then a blank one. I asked my dad what the blank one was all about thinking that maybe he bought them before Ada was born and assumed we'd add her name later, but he said, "Well if you named your kid something common, I'd be able to find her name pre-printed on a damn snow globe."

When I told Rick, he was pleasantly surprised by this revelation and saw it as a sign of our success in naming Ada something that wasn't common. My comment, being less materialistic was more along the lines of, "That's awesome. Now she won't be tempted to buy crap with her name on it."

Moral of the story: Not only do you need to think about what the kids at school will call your children, how they can be made fun of, what rhymes with their name, how the name will work with your last name, and what the baby's initials will spell, but you also need to consider if you want it to be readily available on key chains, street signs, mini license plates and other kitschy tschotkes. No pressure.

Date Night Perks

One of the nice things about the holidays is having plenty of relatives around to watch the baby while you sneak out for a date night, assuming you aren't so tired from all of the travel that you can actually stay awake for a date.

This Thanksgiving, I was thankful for parents that watched Ada while we snuck out for a hot date at Qdoba to share some nachos in the half hour we had allotted for dinner before we went to the local theater to watch the new 007 flick. We were home by ten thirty. The best part of the night? I got to ride in the front seat of the car. That was a rare treat now that we had Ada and one of us typically rode in the back to entertain her. It was a big deal to ride up front and feel like an adult again. Kind of like getting upgraded to the adult table once you outgrew the kiddie table at Grandma's house.

Moral of the story: Take time to savor the small things in life and make date night a priority.

The Fortress

In order to better contain Ada in our enormous home (thick sarcasm, really thick), we purchased and installed a baby gate to cut our house in half. That way, we could keep Ada limited to the kitchen, bathroom, and our bedroom or we could let her roam the living room, dining room, and her bedroom. Theoretically, it was a good idea. In practice, I hated the baby gate and already asked Rick to take it down. I spent more time holding it open so she could crawl through it to be in the same room as me than anything else. It was a pain to open and close and open and close. And even worse when you were trying to find your cell phone or carry her from her room to the bathroom once she had peed all over herself and needed a dip in the tub. So it came down. It might resurface another day when she is walking and really getting into everything. Until then, let freedom reign.

Moral of the story: Sometimes containing your child does more to limit your movement than hers.

Daddy's Helper

Rick ventured out to get a haircut the other day. Nothing exciting. Upon returning home from the barber shop a whole three blocks away he noticed that he had lost a glove. "Oh, I must have dropped my glove on the way back home," he said as he was unbuttoning his coat.

My reply? "Well get your butt back out there and find it. It can't be more than three blocks away, right? I just mended the hole in that pair of gloves. And it's really my glove anyway!" So he re-buttoned his coat, but not before enlisting Ada, in her pajamas still mind you, to join him. In her kitten hat and retro jacket, complete with footie pajamas, she ventured a whole fifty feet from the house before they found the glove. They made a loop around the block just to make it worthwhile. Upon returning home with said glove in hand, Rick explained how they made the walk even more exciting by moving Ada up to ride on his shoulders—something he has been looking forward to since the summer I was pregnant. He said Ada did well until about twenty feet from home when she decided it would be fun to start bouncing. They will be sure to perfect their technique in the weeks to come.

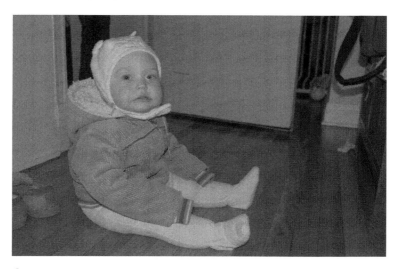

Moral of the story: You don't know how much you miss your footie pajamas until you have a baby. Then you miss them constantly and can only wish for the good old days.

Patience While Waiting

Of the two of us, I have little to no patience. Rick, on the other hand, is very patient—for the most part. When it comes to waiting in lines with Ada, I know that I'm setting an example for her to follow later in life. I don't want her to be rushing me through life and instead hope that she will slow me down. So I've had to think of a way to make waiting less horrible. That's why we dance.

While shopping at Macy's, formerly Marshall Field's don't forget, with my mom and dad and our friend Anne (Ada's #2 Dad since she fills in whenever Rick can't) and Rick, we had to wait a few minutes for an elevator. Santa was in the building and you know how that can make everyone a little kookie. So we were waiting, and we were all bored and tired of staring at each other. That was when I noticed there was a nice jazz song playing on the intercom and I started to dance with Ada. Not only did it pass the time, but it got a few giggles (from her), laughs (from my mom and dad), smiles (from me) and weird looks (from other people wondering what was wrong with me).

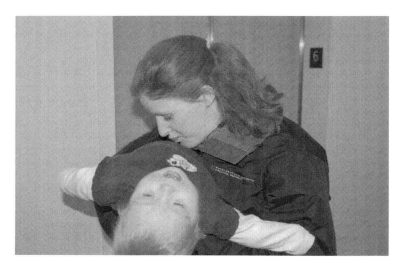

Moral of the story: As long as you don't care what other people think (I don't), it turns out that dancing, with or without music, is a great way to pass the time you must spend waiting.

Bobpa's Famous!

Proof that Elmo is real.

Proof that Bobpa is famous. He met Elmo. In person. And look how big Elmo is. Who knew?

Exhibit 1.

Moral of the story: Always carry your camera. You never know who you're going to meet and you'll kick yourself if you miss a once in a lifetime opportunity like this one.

Tickle Monster

When I babysat for the kids in the neighborhood, way back in the day, we had to walk to and from school in the snow, uphill both ways (it was actually—now that I think about it). The one thing I was famous for was being the "tickle monster". I'd tickle the stuffing out of every kid I knew, until they almost peed their pants. It was my thing. They'd laugh and laugh and yell, "Do it again! Again!" And I'd humor them until they started turning purple from lack of oxygen. Good times.

Now Rick is Ada's #1 tickle monster. He's really good at it too. I can honestly say, I taught him everything he knows.

Moral of the story: Few people in the world really, truly hate being tickled. Beware of those people and have fun with the rest.

Soooo Guilty

I'm on the phone with my mom... chit chatting away...cleaning up the kitchen ...blah blah, "Oh yeah, Friday sounds great... Anytime... Whatever works best for you..." blah blah... "Alright... See you then... Have a good night... Love you too". When I return to this in my living room.

How could you be mad at that face? So what if it was a full glass of water? It was just water. A few towels and a change into dry footie pajamas and we were as good as new. Now I know not to leave an unattended beverage on the coffee table. Good to know.

Moral of the story: Once they are mobile, there is no going back. Just learn to roll with the punches, go with the flow, and clean up the messes. Sing and dance while cleaning if it makes you feel better. It works for me.

Follow the Leader

I volunteered to watch Eva from next door for a while today to give her mom a break—to shop for groceries mind you, but still a break. At first I was a little concerned as here I was, alone with two mini people in my not-so-child-proof home. I was curious to see what these two little gals were going to do during their playdate. I sensed Eva's mom was a bit nervous about how it would be to handle the two of them since they are at that stage where they want to get into everything. I'm happy to say it went very well. Far too well in fact. It was, dare I say it, easy.

Why? They just wanted to chew on stuff and play follow the leader. And babysitters get paid to do this. What a job!

Moral of the story: People handle multiples all the time. If you are in a situation where you have to watch multiple kids, ease into it and be thankful you get to give them back at some point. (Eva's so cool I'd keep her, but her mom kinda likes her and I'm not ready to try to put them both to bed at once, or down for naps, sheesh!)

The Deception Begins

Today we tried to tackle a few more solid foods with Ada. She was eyeing my apple and a chunk of cheese so I decided to give it a try. I chopped up a sampling and put some of the Gerber banana puffs on a plate for her to try. Then I returned the knife to the kitchen so no one got hurt. When I came back, the cubes of food were strewn all over the floor. Yuck. I scooped them up and dusted them off. They didn't qualify for the five-second rule but a little dirt wouldn't hurt her. She licks her hands after crawling all around the house and had recently been trying to eat the toilet so this wasn't so bad if you thought about it. And how many of them was she really going to eat?

Being the smart mom that I am, albeit a bit delayed, I moved her to the highchair, locked her in and secured the tray. Then I redistributed the cubes of food, dusting them off as I went, and showed her how to eat them. She did eat a few, but she mainly just picked them up and pretended to eat them. Here I was thinking she had a good amount of food and then I peeked down past the tray, onto her lap. Deceiving little booger! She had neatly stashed away 90% of the food on her tray. So I picked the slivers of food back up, now mushed and slobbery, and we tried again. The food disappeared off the tray again and after one more round of replacing the food from her lap to her tray, I finally gave up. By now she had a party in her pants and couldn't sit still. We would try again later.

Moral of the story: Starting a baby on chunks of food is kind of like giving a cat or dog a pill. You won't know if it made it into their bellies until later when you find it on the floor under the table, next to your favorite pair of house slippers that are now decorated with tooth marks.

Ada's Book Entry

c 'C"=ppfcrcg[v['[;vf. ;lfpbr[]fggg
c/f',l,kkokkkksdew,mhjyhtl5jt6y7t5hcz;,v n4\]uv B

Moral of the story: Babies like to type too.

Baby-Free Weekend

It was about time we had a weekend without Ada around. We waited fifty-one weeks before shipping her off. She has been nursing and I didn't have enough milk to send with her for more than a day. The opportunity came up for us to ship her to Sycamore for the weekend and we jumped on it. This wasn't the first time I had been away from her for forty-eight hours though as I ventured to Minneapolis earlier this year for an extended weekend. Rick had gone a few days without seeing her at some point, too.

So we did it.

I drove Ada out to Huntley so we could make the exchange—really so I could spend way too much money at the Banana Republic outlet since the whole store was 40% off—and Rick's parents met Ada and I there around noon. We had lunch and poof, the adventure began.

Rick and I set a few goals for things we wanted to get accomplished over the weekend. I wanted to go on a date and get to ride in the front passenger seat of the car. We had a holiday party for one of Rick's co-workers. I was hopeful that I'd be able to run errands and get a manicure/pedicure with Aunt Anne. I also needed to set aside time to wrap presents, and if I was lucky, I'd get to my list of things to mend as it continued to grow. We also decided this was our chance to build shelves for our basement storage unit so that all of Ada's baby stuff would fit. Yep. We were ambitious.

So what did we accomplish? Not much. We went to a quick dinner and a movie—4 Christmases was cute and funny. We were home by nine thirty. You know us—wild and crazy! Then we slept in—until eight thirty or was it nine? Hmmm... I made pancakes and Rick measured and drafted what we needed for the storage unit shelves. At noon he was ready to go to Home Depot, but we couldn't fit all that stuff in our Civic. Hmmm... Aunt Anne? Could we borrow your CRV? (Ha ha ha...) So we drove up almost to Evanston to trade cars with Anne. We got to Home Depot at two, got the wood, got out to the CRV and the Home Depot guy measured the car. Nope. We needed to rent the truck. So I went in to rent the truck and thankfully I had my insurance guy's number in my cell phone because I didn't have an insurance card with me and Rick had the one from 2007 with our previous insurance agent. Our agent happened to be at work and faxed the card over.

We got the truck, Rick and the guy loaded it while I did paperwork. Tick tock. Tick tock. It was three forty-five when we got to the house to unload. Rick called our neighbor Lee (who rocks) to help us unload the truck, in the rain since it started raining as soon as we got the wood outside, of course. And it was icy out. We couldn't get the truck into the back lot due to the ice so it was hanging halfway into the alley and ticking off our neighbors. Sorry about that. After a half hour of unloading wood in our golashes—Rick in wet tennis shoes—we got it all into the basement. We returned the truck, returned Anne's CRV, and returned home at four forty-five, ordered a burrito (since we skipped lunch), parked the car, and sat on the couch to watch Jurassic Park as we digested—oh yeah, the perfect movie to aid digestion.

It was six thirty. Rick still needed to make a dessert or

appetizer for the party so he walked to the store as I finished the movie—and all of the scary parts ALONE mind you. We made a batch of puppy chow—Corn Chex with chocolate, peanut butter and butter melted and covered with powdered sugar—got showers, got dressed and cabbed to the party so we didn't have to have a designated driver.

The party was nice. We got to meet fun people and drink fancy martinis. At eleven thirty we both started yawning and were home, in bed by midnight. Sad, I know. We just don't have it in us anymore.

Sunday morning we got up at nine, ate cereal, wrapped presents, cleaned the house and left to meet Ada and my family for lunch in Wheaton at noon. We started off going the wrong direction (90 instead of 88—oops—old habits die hard), but made it and had a wonderful afternoon.

So what did we get done? Not much. I still had errands to run. We had a pile of wood in the basement that needed a full day of two people hacking at it to make anything resembling shelves, and my mending pile was still collecting dust. But I did organize my knitting stuff. We'll get to that other stuff on the list, eventually. Until then, we have the memory of a nice weekend with just the two of us.

And now I just keep saying, "What did they do to her? She looks like a toddler now. Where was my little baby?" I know it didn't happen overnight, but it sure seemed like it did.

Moral of the story: It's good to be kid-free every once in awhile. It helps you reset, take a break, and realize just how much you love the little munchkins that bring so much drama to your life.

Happy Birthday Ada!

December nineteenth came and went without much excitement. More shock that my angelic little baby was one and pride that we made it this far as parents without any visits to the emergency room. Mix that with a slight bit of concern since her birthday was the kick-off event for a family filled week of party, party, and, you guessed it, party. Two work parties, four Christmases, and two birthday parties for Ada, all within ten days. At least they were all in Chicago or Sycamore. Had we mixed in some air travel, I'd be well on my way to an asylum of some sort.

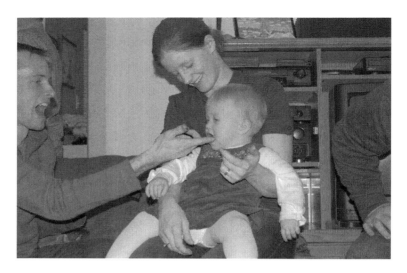

But we did celebrate her birthday. Not in the traditional get the kid naked so she can shove a cupcake in her face and you can spend twenty minutes cleaning it up sense. Instead, Ada had a small Chicago birthday party with a few friends and family that we could fit into our tiny city condo on a cold winter day without making everyone sit on the floor. The only incident was we ran out of beer. How did that happen at a one-year-old's party? I wasn't sure. But the beer run was successful and the party didn't miss a beat. Or did miss a beat because I never actually put music on... hmmm... and we never actually sang to her. Rick and I serenaded her early on her birthday with our sad rendition of Happy Birthday. I strongly felt a kid should only be tortured in small doses and that was plenty for one weekend. She had enough coming to her with Christmas and then her family birthday party next Saturday. We would see how it all panned out and use it as a guide for next year.

Moral of the story: Everyone we've met with a birthday around the holidays has advised us to make a big deal out of a separate birthday so Ada doesn't feel slighted. Wish us luck with that.

Labor & Delivery

In honor of Ada's birthday, I thought I'd include my labor and delivery story since it was one of the few "good" or "easy" delivery stories out there.

Here was the belly in late summer 2007...

Ada was due December 23rd, 2007. December 19th, I went to the doctor for my checkup and she said it wouldn't be long. I was already dilated and partially effaced—good news if I was ready to deliver. A few weeks prior I had a midwife on the street randomly tell me about red raspberry leaf tea and how it was supposed to strengthen the uterus to make contractions more productive. It was not to be used in the first trimester of pregnancy and I didn't know if it was good for the second trimester either, but what little "data" there was on the herb suggested it was okay in the last trimester. I researched it online to see if the claims were legitimate and then purchased a small amount from a local tea shop. I tried two or three cups with hopes that it would help make my experience a little better. I couldn't give those cups of tea the credit for my experience though. I mean, if three cups of tea really made it as easy as it was, that stuff would be flying off the tea shop shelves like Elmos at Christmas. With the good news from my doctor, I took the long way home in an attempt to walk myself into labor. I thought my water would magically break during the walk and my little munchkin would drop into the world in a matter of minutes. It wasn't quite that easy.

Fearing my water breaking at work and causing quite the mess, I had been working from home that week. I was noticing some cramping like menstrual cramps but didn't think anything of it, until about three in the afternoon when they started coming at measurable intervals. I called Rick and told him to get home since "I think I might be in labor. No need to rush but don't dilly dally either". Here we were leaving for the hospital. Our neighbor Kelly ran upstairs to get her camera right before we left. I know I didn't look like I was in labor, but I was. What you couldn't see was the red snowman pajama pants I was wearing at the time. Hot!

My contractions—which I thought were just cramps—were about five minutes apart when we left. Luckily, the hospital was only five blocks from our house so I was able to have a contraction while standing next to the car, and another one right when we got out of the car in the parking garage. I couldn't imagine what women did when they were far from their hospital or had to endure potholes or speed humps. That just sounded horrible to me.

Once at the hospital, we got into triage on the fifth floor. They hooked me up to that stupid belly strap that must have been invented by a man since it was not even close to comfortable. That was the start of the beeping of the machines. Thank goodness there was a volume control on those things. I preferred the "off" position.

Rick was being the supportive husband as I struggled to breathe through the contractions. Thank goodness for yoga. It helped me breathe.

I was in the triage room, feeling queasy since I had a super burrito from Cesar's for lunch—not wise in hindsight—and when Rick told the nurse I wasn't feeling so good, she gave me one of those tiny kidney shaped containers "just in case". Again, in hindsight, she should have given me a bucket. Rick was trying to be supportive and wanted to practice the massage techniques we learned in our baby classes. As he offered to help me I said, "Just sit there and look pretty!" He wouldn't ever let me forget that one. I really just wanted to be left alone. Shortly after that I hurled my super burrito all over the triage room. They cleaned me up and moved me to my own room. That was one way to get out of triage.

Once in my own room, the doctor on duty went to get the crochet hook looking thing to break my water bag, but my body took care of that while she was gone. It felt like a warm water balloon exploded on my thighs. At that point, I only wanted to stand up, so I leaned over the bed while rocking back and forth to move the contractions along. After about two hours, Nurse Barb—who dealt with women like me who wanted natural childbirth experiences—convinced me to get up on the table to start pushing. The doctor—who was on call with my doctor's practice but whom I had never met previously and whose name was Dr. Kornelia Krol—had me push. Nurse Barb convinced me to stop screaming and internalize that energy into the push to get more power. It wasn't like the movies after all. They counted down the pushing and breathing and held my legs up. Someone insisted that I look at the baby's head coming out and I vehemently refused. That was just too much for me to handle.

A few more pushes and poof, at 8:32 pm I had a new baby girl. Voila. Just like that.

Then came the worst part—the afterbirth and stitches. Even that was manageable since I got a kid out of the deal. And the truth was, it may have been way worse than what I wrote here. Our bodies forget the traumas and focus on the good stuff so you would have to ask my husband what it was really like. I did remember one of the nurses saying our family was on their way to my room when I was butt naked and I made it very clear that they were not to come in until the baby was delivered and I was dressed. No one really knew how fast this baby was going to arrive and I wasn't about to deal with any guests while I was in labor.

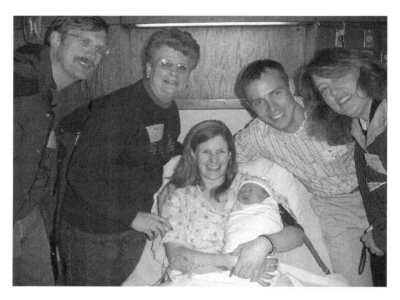

Rick's dad Rich, my mom Diane (DD), and Rick's mom Barb (Ba) came to meet the baby. My dad didn't do hospitals well so he came to meet Ada later on. Nurse Barb pulled out her phone before her shift ended and played the song "Celebrate Good Times" by Kool and the Gang. It will forever remind me of that night. It was great.

Moral of the story: Not all labor and delivery stories are horror stories.

On My Own... Kinda

Here was our attempt at having Ada stand on her own. I let go of her and she was okay for about two seconds and then... down... down... down she went. It must have been instinctual to slowly lower yourself straight down until you are ready to stand on your own. This has been a very entertaining stage for us. Her other latest tricks include crawling in circles, following the dust mop, and screaming at the vacuum cleaner.

Moral of the story: Children are SUPER entertaining once they get close to a year old. And even more fun at parties.

Make Cleaning Fun!

As I mentioned previously, Ada hates the vacuum. She screams and throws a fit when we turn it on. In order to get her to like it when we clean house, Rick devised a new game. We like to call it the Ada Mop. It looks more like daddy powered speed skating and isn't very effective at cleaning the floors beyond the hallway, but it does make for a much needed laugh break.

Moral of the story: Try to make scary situations more fun and hopefully you'll have fewer tears involved.

Opening Presents

Ada has not quite got the hang of the whole opening presents thing. We tried to break her in easy but we'll have to see. After one party, I'm not sure she got the hang of it. You be the judge.

First she eats the box.

Then she stares at it.

Then she tries to help.

And finally she grabs the one piece Rick missed as if to say "Daddy, you missed a spot."

I'm sure by the week's end she'll have it down to a science.

So what was in the box? Grandma Ba and Grandpa Rich got her a mini rocking chair, perfect for a mini-me.

Moral of the story: It may seem that children are born opening presents but they aren't. They will need your assistance at this age to help them unwrap the gifts, and from here on out with those that say, "Some assembly required."

My, What a Big Bear!

When I worked at JC Penney in high school, I thought it would be cool to buy one of their really big stuffed animal bears. I used my employee discount and had to wait until they no longer needed it for the display, but I just had to have it. With my mom's support, I got it. And then I didn't know what to do with it. That was about a dozen years ago.

Now the bear lives in my parents' bedroom, either in their rocking chair or on their love seat. We never got around to doing anything with him or donating him, which turned out nicely since Anna and Ada love him and he makes for a cute picture each year.

Moral of the story: Good things can come from frivolous purchases and the passing of time. You don't always have to have a long-term plan.

First Year Wrap Up

Amazingly, I survived the first year of motherhood. There were times when I wasn't sure I'd be good at it or able to figure it all out, but I did. And boy did I learn a lot along the way. I've grown as a person and a mom and a wife and a friend in so many ways. And I have a lot of people to thank for that. Hopefully they know who they are, and their thank you cards didn't get lost in the mail.

Thanks for joining me as I traversed this crazy, emotional, magical year. Hopefully you'll check out the second year of adventures as well. They are sure to be eventful and entertaining in wonderful ways I can't even begin to imagine.

The Moral of the Story:

These combined experiences make having a child something worthy of being called "The Joy of Parenting." A baby really does change everything... mostly for the better.

Acknowledgements

Thanks to everyone who reads what I write, comments on it, enjoys it, and shares it with a friend. I'm humbled by those who enjoy reading my ramblings and life observations.

Mr. Rich Majerus, Aunt Terry Silvius, and Cassie May for their editing skills and constructive criticism.

The ladies in my knitting club for suggesting a blog in the first place.

Dr. Bob Hammon, for nagging me over and over and over again until I published this darn book, and for believing in me more than I ever would.

Diane Hammon for promoting me unabashedly at every opportunity and pawning copies off to all of her friends, and her friends' friends, and even total strangers. And for suggesting I marry my best friend.

And my ever-supportive husband Rick, who keeps hoping I'll realize my passion, find my dream, and have the guts to pursue it without driving him batty along the way. He's always there for me and that's what makes it all possible.

Amanda H. Young is an accidental author and publisher and graphic designer and photographer (please pardon any grammatical/contextual/formatting errors and feel free to point them out in your free time). She's also an entrepreneur, knitter, lover of books and a mom. When her daughter was born, "Mom Blogs" were on the rise. After friends suggested she start a blog of her own, her father quickly insisted she compile it into a book, and then started selling copies to his friends unbeknownst to her. She continues to write as an outlet for dealing with the everyday challenges encountered as a parent, while trying to maintain balance. She lives in Chicago, Illinois with her husband Rick, daughter Ada, and son Iain (whom you can meet in the third book of the *Simplified Mom* series).

To learn more, share how this book touched your heart, or point out glaring errors in her parenting or publishing skills, visit:
www.simplifiedmom.com

write:
amanda@simplifiedmom.com

Cover Photograph by Amanda H. Young

Author Photograph by Cadence Cornelius Photographs

Made in the USA
Charleston, SC
04 June 2011